A HACKER NO MORE

The Step-By-Step Guide to
Bringing Your Game Up to Par

By William C. Kroen,
author of the best-selling **The Why Book of Golf**

A HACKER NO MORE

by

William C. Kroen

Copyright © 1987, 1993 by William C. Kroen
Published by Price Stern Sloan, Inc.
11150 Olympic Boulevard
Los Angeles, CA 90064
Printed in the United States of America

10 9 8 7 6 5 4 3 2 1

Library of Congress Cataloging in Publication

Kroen, William C.
    A Hacker no more : relearning your way to par / by William C. Kroen.
       p. cm.
    ISBN 0-8431-3470-4
    1. Golf. I. Title.
GV965.K744   1993   92-37306
796.352—dc20   CIP

Photography by George Loring.

ACKNOWLEDGMENTS

To my mother and father and the loving memory of my mother-in-law, Mrs. Katherine Coady Boyle.

I wish to thank Bruce Hoster and Sandra Fraser of Dunlop Slazenger Corporation and Mark Bisbing of Nike for their assistance and continued support. A special thanks is due to Corrine Johnson, my editor, whose talent and expertise were invaluable to me. In particular, I wish to thank my wife, Kathy, and daughters, Kerry and Kristen, for their love and encouragement.

TABLE OF CONTENTS

Introduction

Several years ago, while driving home from the golf course, I spotted a bumper sticker that read, Am I Having Fun? While humorous to some people, it was a serious question to me in regard to my golf game. Golf was supposed to be fun—sunshine, good friends, fresh air and a sense of accomplishment at hitting a good golf shot. Yet at that particular time in my golfing life, golf had become more a source of anger and frustration.

I had picked up the game as a caddy and steadily improved to the point where I played on teams in college and in the Marine Corps. Yet at my best I was not better than an 80s shooter despite hours and hours of practice. As I became a weekend golfer my game deteriorated to the point where I had difficulty breaking 90. My expectations were always high, but bad shot would follow bad shot in a frustrating cycle. As I continued to play poorly, I finally asked myself the bumper sticker question. I was not really having fun. I was ruining my Saturdays and Sundays by spending four or five hours cursing myself. The frustration and embarrassment at playing so poorly took its toll. I finally did the only logical thing—I quit. I would play only two or three times per year, shoot a 95 and tell myself, "Now I remember just why I quit!"

In other parts of my life I had been successful, yet on the golf course I was a failure. Golf is the Rubik's Cube™ of games. Hard work and effort do not necessarily translate into success. The golfer stands alone on the course in his own vulnerability. Each slice or shank is a reflection of his or her incompetence. There is no one else to blame, no quarterback who overthrew a receiver, no catcher who let the ball get by him. The golfer exposes his ability on every shot and then has time to brood and incriminate himself until the next shot. In a way, the game seems to be structured as a form of slow torture for the poor golfer.

Yet golf addiction runs deep. As I sat home on beautiful Saturdays and Sundays, I knew that I could not stay away from the game for long. Several years ago I decided to give the game one more try. I made a vow to myself that if I were going to play the game at all, it would be as a very good golfer and not as the hacker that I had been.

I had two masters degrees and a Ph.D. in the areas of psychology and education. I decided to approach the relearning of the game based on the sound principles that I had acquired in these fields. I devised and set in motion a plan in which I would relearn every aspect of the game from scratch. I set goals and objectives for myself that were not in terms of scores but in terms of mastery of the many skills, abilities and attitudes involved in the game of golf.

My first step was to thoroughly research the game. I read over twenty five instruction books, watched every instruction video possible, interviewed pros and duffers and made clinical observations. Clinical observation goes well beyond the simple watching of a golf swing—it involves a scrupulous investigation of detail. My clinical observations extended from the touring pro to the hacker. I wanted to dissect every aspect of the game and make comparisons of what caused success and failure. My frustration and anger at not being able to master this game drove me to the same level of intensity I would have had trying to find a cure for a dreaded disease.

In the field of education, total learning is thought to encompass three domains—cognitive, affective and psychomotor. The cognitive domain deals with knowledge, the "how-to" of golf. The affective domain involves the acquiring of attitudes, emotional control and discipline. The psychomotor aspect deals with the relationship of brain impulses to our bodily movements. To become a complete golfer I made up my mind to approach the learning of the game from these three standpoints.

After one year of my program the results surprised even me. In a period of eight days I played five rounds at my home course with a worst score of 74. I had never scored a 74 in my life on that course, and I had to stop and pause to reflect on the change that had come about. I remember coming home and telling my wife that it didn't seem that it was really me who was playing this well. The golf shots that were coming off my clubs consistently seemed foreign to me. In effect, I had, through hard work and dedication, become a completely different person on the golf course. The change did not come overnight, but it was indeed real and quite dramatic.

A Hacker No More is a step-by-step guide to my transformation. I will share the insights, observations and training techniques that enabled me to become a good golfer. I will enable you, the reader, to answer with a resounding "yes" when you ask yourself if you are having fun on the golf course.

1

CHANGE

As a teacher and coach, I have the opportunity to work with young people on a daily basis. It never ceases to amaze me how quickly youngsters are able to pick up a new skill or concept and master it. At the same time, however, I am often called upon to give workshops and lectures to adult groups. Often I will come away from these sessions asking myself, "Why is it so difficult to get a point across to these people? They are intelligent and well-educated, but there always seems to be resistance present." The answer is relatively simple: it lies in the area of development and is rooted in the ability to change.

Children are constantly in a change mode. They expect change and welcome it. They possess a subconscious awareness that they need to be open and receptive to change in order to acquire the skills and abilities necessary to grow and function successfully. Young children can master a foreign language in one year while adults will struggle for a lifetime. As parents, we have all experienced the "terrible twos," during which our two-year-olds all but destroy a house trying to explore their environment. Then, as three- and four-year-olds, they drive us crazy with endless questions. These are just part of a normal development pattern for a child to learn about life. The child is an "active learner" who is more than ready, willing and able to absorb all that he or she can in order to grow.

As an adult, things become different. We tend to fall into a comfort zone both mentally and physically. Things that move us out of the comfort zone—new ideas, for example—are not always met with open arms. We tend to stay with what is comfortable, whether it is our political views or a golf swing. Change is consciously and subconsciously resisted. Beginning medical students learn that the body has built-in mechanisms designed to resist change and return the system to normal. It is not so preposterous to assume that our minds also possess mechanisms that resist change. MBA students learn that even corporations subconsciously develop mechanisms that resist change and that it will often require outside intervention to bring about substantial change for an institution.

What does this have to do with learning the game of golf? If you are going to make a substantial improvement in your golf game, you must substantially change both your physical and mental approach to the game. When I was at the bottom of my game, I had a wide assortment of bad shots in my repertoire. Hook, slice, top, shank—you name it, I did it. No simple change such as moving my left hand over on my grip or opening my stance was suddenly going to transform me into a good golfer. In my golfing life I had tried every method of improvement short of a visit to Lourdes. I came to the realization that in order to become a good golfer I had to become an active learner who was open and receptive to the changes that would be required.

By reading, study and observation I built a solid knowledge base. Much of this book is a compilation of the knowledge that I acquired. While essential, knowledge by itself is not enough to transform a poor golfer into a good one. By listening to and reading about Mozart we do not become great composers. By taking the knowledge base and combining it with sound learning strategies and attitudinal change, I was able to put together a comprehensive package of learning that would bring about real improvement. The key was to become almost childlike in my approach to learning by being open and receptive to ideas and willing to accept change along the way.

Before we get into swing mechanics and proper golf thinking, I think that it is important to take a look at what learning is and what it takes to be a good learner.

John Dewey, often referred to as "The Father of American Education," defined learning as that which is internalized or "made our own." It is taking a skill, concept or attitude and absorbing it into our psyche in a way that it becomes part of our very makeup. Dewey also stressed that a critical component of learning is that the learner be an "active learner." For the golfer, this does not just mean beating balls and playing a lot of rounds. Many golfers get progressively worse despite the amount of time they devote to golf and simply chalk it up to being in a slump of growing older. An active learner is one who is receptive to ideas and change, is committed to mastering the required skills and sees learning as a continuous process.

We live in a television society where most problems are solved in thirty- or sixty-minute time frames. How many times have you heard a golfer tell about making a slight change in his grip that completely changed his game? Let's face it, worthwhile learning on our road to becoming a good golfer is going to be gradual. There are no overnight cures, but there is definitely a way to become a solid golfer over a reasonable period of time. You can become a good golfer, a very good golfer, if you become an active learner and make up your mind to:

- Be willing to accept change in your physical and mental approach to the game.

- Be patient in learning one skill at a time as a step toward mastering the game of golf.

- Be committed to worthwhile practice routines.

- Allow time for reflection, inventory and self-analysis.

- Set yourself into a learning mode, ready to absorb ideas and techniques that will help you reach your goal.

As you embark on your program of improvement, I think it is important to think about change itself. All of our physical and mental systems tend to resist change. Psychologists have found that change, whether good or bad, will produce high levels of anxiety. Marriage/divorce, birth/death and hired/fired all cause increased stress. Our bodies and minds naturally seek an equilibrium, a comfortable center. In learning golf you will experience times where you will feel awkward and uncomfortable. This is where being an active learner, open to ideas, comes into play. Accept the change, trust it and work at it.

How does this apply to golf in particular? Golf, unlike most learning that we have experienced, is often taught in the negative and in reverse for skill development. Most of us started with the whole swing theory. At some point in our lives, we placed a ball on the ground, picked up a club, took a full swing and whacked at it. Many golf manuals for juniors advocate letting the kids smack the ball for the first few years and then work on the swing later. But from the first time we whacked away at the ball, we have been bombarded with "Don'ts" and "Keeps."

"Don't pick up your head."

"Don't sway."

"Don't try to kill it."

"Keep your left arm straight."

"Keep your right elbow in."

Most of us started with a poor swing at first. This became our normal status, our equilibrium. Each "Don't" and "Keep" worked on our equilibrium over the years for better or worse until our present swings evolved.

Golf is one of the few activities in life where we learn the fundamentals and spend the rest of our learning time correcting faults. It is little wonder that many touring pros are the sons and daughters of professionals and grew up under the guidance of a skilled professional. The fact that most of us started with bad habits does not preclude the capability of making substantial improvement regardless of age. Consider your bad experiences on the golf course as water under the bridge. Bad golf shots in your past serve no value in developing a solid golf game. As you change your swing and mental approach to the game, you will become a different golfer from the one you once knew.

Many instructional golf books suggest playing within your capability and developing a swing based on your ability. To play within your capabilities is sound advice. I would not try to cut a dogleg 250 yards from the tee because I know that I do not have that kind of capability. I do not agree, however, with settling on an ability level as a lease for improvement. As a teacher I

A Hacker No More

often encourage my students to reach beyond their ability levels. By having my students reach beyond, but not so far that they reach the frustration level, I enable them to gain a greater sense of achievement and confidence. As you make up your mind to become a good golfer, raise the expectation level of your own ability—avoid the comfort zone. As you experience success you will find that improvement is progressive. As you hit good shots your confidence level will rise and result in more good shots. Compared to the ability to sense proper swing mechanics and maintain proper thought patterns, size, strength and athletic ability are relatively unimportant to playing good golf.

As you begin to relearn the game, be on guard not to overload yourself with too many concepts. Much of the golf literature today seems to be overwhelming for the average golfer. "Creating a power arc," "forty-five-degree pronation of the wrists" and "eighty-twenty weight distribution" are all examples of worthwhile concepts that can cause an overload of change factors in our swing equilibrium. They may become important to you some time down the road, but in general these are of little value to the guy headed out of Hackersville.

As you read through the instructions of this book try to absorb concepts in small bits. I have tried to give not only the *hows* and *whys* of golf mechanics but also a sense of how each movement feels. It is the relationship between how a proper swing is executed and how it feels to you that is at the root of acquiring the required skills.

Hitting a golf ball is a skill made up of many parts called sub-skills. Riding a bike, driving a car and throwing a ball are all examples of skills that we have learned in an ordered sequence of mastering the sub-skills. When you learned to read, chances are you followed a progression of associating objects with words, learning the vowel sounds, then the sounds that come from blending letters. You were set on a course of progression based on mastery of the sub-skills involved in reading. As you read this page, you have no conscious thought of the many sub-skills that you are employing. In golf we need to master the sub-skills in a manner that will enable us to make a smooth, efficient swing that is produced on command.

Your ability to change and improve will be mostly determined by your commitment to learning. There have been several average club golfers who have made it to the PGA Tour in a matter of a few years. While this is certainly an exceptional achievement, it does serve to point out the range of human potential to change and improve in golf. Recognize the fact that there is a good golfer within your capability. Work toward bringing about change and accept it.

2

THE GRIP

The logical place to begin your make-over is the grip. When I set out to change my game, I looked to the touring professionals first. I studied stop-action photos and videotapes and watched the players in person at PGA tournaments. I approached my observations as a clinician. In other words, I carefully studied every aspect of their golf swings, noting the intricacies and patterns of every swing. I found that there was a relatively large range of swing places, swing speeds, tempos, stances and bodily movements. Two areas, however, jumped out at me as being common threads that ran through these great golfers' approaches to hitting the ball: 1) the position at impact and 2) the grip. It didn't take a genius to realize that if the top 150 golfers out of 18 million all used essentially the same grip, then there must be something very important about how they hold the club.

Just stop and think for a minute about what the grip does in the golf swing:

- Your hands are the only part of your body that touches the club. Your shoulder-turn, hip movement, foot action—everything you do in your swing—is transmitted to the clubhead through your grip.

- The grip controls how the face of the club squares to the ball. What this means in terms of accuracy is that on a drive of 250 yards, a clubface opened just five degrees would produce a shot 50 yards off-target. Don't let this scare you. A proper grip will enable you to start square and return the clubface square like a well-oiled machine.

- The grip allows for (or restricts) the free movement of the rest of your body.

A good grip will provide the quickest and most rewarding change that you will experience in developing your new approach to the game. The proper grip will allow you to return the clubface to the ball squarely time after time, increasing your distance because of greater freedom of movement and giving you a feeling of control and confidence that translates into success. The grip is so essential to good golf that I often tell the good player from the hacker by simply looking at how he holds the club.

Most of us will never have the great swings of the touring pros, but we can have their grip. Remember, your new grip may feel a little awkward at first. This is all part of learning and change, and there will be a period of adjustment as you correct the way you hold the club. It is for this very reason that young kids can pick up the game quickly while adults struggle to acquire the same skills. My old grip was very comfortable, and I never gave it much thought. Once I realized it was at the root of many of my problems, I made the necessary changes and experienced surprising improvement. Your new grip will not only feel comfortable in time but will be the starting block for real gains.

The Proper Grip

Rather than begin with a description of how to lay your hands on the club properly, I think it is important to first talk about the correct pressure of the grip. While the grip is responsible for many things, its main purpose is to provide a way of allowing a hinge action for our wrists. The amount of pressure that you exert on the grip directly affects your wrist movement as you swing back and then down and through the ball.

The gripping action of your hands and fingers is controlled by muscle groups in your forearms. To prove this, squeeze the under part of your right forearm with your left hand. Now try to make a fist. You will notice that your hand and finger muscles are restricted. A grip that creates tension in your forearms will prevent you from making a smooth takeaway during the backswing and a strong, accurate move on the downswing toward impact. Additionally, the tight-fingered grip causes other muscle groups to tense, which produces a jerky movement and restricts the swing.

My problem was that I had a death grip on the club with my left hand. I did this with the false notion that it would give me more power from a firm left side. In reality, I was robbing myself of power by restricting the free flow of the clubhead in my hands. As a high school baseball coach, I would tell my pitchers to look at the hands of the batter. If the batter was "white-knuckling" the bat the pitcher would hold the ball as long as possible before making his delivery. By the time the ball was pitched the batter would have expended energy and built up tension in his arms and hands that would, in effect, produce a restricted swing. The same principle holds true for the golf grip.

When I grip the club now I check to see if the muscles in my forearms are flexed and tense. I make sure my forearms are soft. As you swing the club you will naturally hold the club with the required pressure. The key is to start with a grip that makes you feel as if no muscles in your body are tensed. At first, you may feel that you are too loose. Trust me on this one. By holding the club softly and in an address position that is completely relaxed, you are putting yourself in a position to make a smooth-flowing swing. The soft grip will allow a better feel of the clubhead. The golf swing is actually a slinging action in which the clubhead is pulled rather than pushed along its path.

Types of Grips

There are three basic grips used today in golf: the overlapping, the interlocking and the ten-finger. You should try all three to see which one provides a comfortable feeling of control for you. Note that each grip is described from a right-handed perspective. For left-handed players, the hands will be reversed.

The Overlapping. The overlapping or Vardon grip is the one used by the majority of professionals and top amateurs. This does not automatically mean that it is the best grip for you as individual differences will dictate your preferences. This grip is characterized by the little finger of the right hand nuzzling into the crevice created between the first and second fingers of the left hand (*see figure 1*). This grip should give you a feeling of oneness as the hands work together. It should give you flexibility in your wrists. These feelings become important in the moves that you will have to make in the backswing and downswing. This grip is best for players who have strong hands and good control of the finger muscles. I find this grip to be the most comfortable and easiest to execute correctly.

The Interlocking. The interlocking grip is the next most popular grip among golfers. It is characterized by the placement of the little finger of the right hand between the first and second fingers of the left hand. The little finger of the right hand is actually locked between the first and second fingers of the left hand (*see figure 2*). Many players find that this interlocking of the fingers helps them to keep the right hand on the club at the top of the swing much better than with the overlapping grip. This grip should also produce a feeling of having the hands work together on the club. Players with small hands tend to prefer this grip.

figure 1

figure 2

A Hacker No More

The Ten-Finger. The ten-finger or baseball grip is just what its name implies. All ten fingers are on the club the way they would be when holding a baseball bat. This grip is often preferred by youngsters who are starting out because it gives a greater sense of control during the swing. To me, however, this grip tends to give the feeling of the hands working against each other. While there are great golfers who use this grip, I would recommend the overlapping or interlocking for the golfer seeking improvement. If you use the ten-finger grip now, try the other grips, develop a feel for them and see if you can adapt one to your game.

Gripping the Club

It is important that you make the proper gripping of the club a checkpoint in your pre-shot routine. Develop the habit of gripping the club the correct way and in the same sequence every time you step up to the ball. By setting aside a few seconds every time, you will avoid becoming sloppy or careless in the way you hold the club. Often such things as club selection or wind conditions will distract you from the proper amount of attention that the grip deserves. From practice and repetition you will eventually develop to the point where the feel of the club in your hands indicates to you whether or not you are holding the club correctly. I still make a check of my grip each time as a matter of habit.

I use the following sequence in gripping the club:

- Stand up straight with both hands at your sides and the club held loosely in your left hand.

- Lay the sole of the club on the ground in front of you so that it lies flat. The clubface should be square to your target line. Many times I have seen high handicappers grip the club while the clubhead is in the air. There is no way that they can assure that the clubface is square and that the hands are in the proper position on the club.

- Let the grip of the club run across your left palm from the inside knuckle of your first finger to the pad or fleshy part of your hand. The fleshy part of the hand is actually a strong muscle that plays an important role in the grip. It is this muscle that holds the club solidly at the top of the swing. I used to hold the club in the fingers of my left hand. Consequently, this grip caused me to lose control of the club at the critical top position. Even though the club feels secure in your fingers as you address the ball, it is impossible to maintain the grip this way during the full swing. By moving the grip into the pad of my left hand, I no longer had to worry about losing the club at the top because of my fingers giving out. At first this change felt awkward, but after a few days of practice I had to wonder how I ever hit the ball with my finger grip.

- Roll your left hand over on top of the shaft and place your thumb so that it is at the "one o'clock" position on the shaft (*see figure 3*). Make sure that you do not place the thumb straight down the shaft as this will cause restrictive movement of the wrists. Extend the thumb so that it rests naturally on the club, neither stretched out nor notched up.

- Place your right hand on the club by interlocking or overlapping your little finger first, then roll your hand over gently to the top of the shaft (*see figure 4*). Be careful not to make any twisting or grabbing motions as this will throw the clubface off of a square alignment.

- Place your right thumb so that it points to the "eleven o'clock" position on the shaft. Let the thumb lie naturally on the club. Again, guard against running the thumb straight down the shaft.

Use the following keys to double-check your grip:

- The gaps between your thumbs and forefingers should form a crease or "V." The Vs of both hands should point to the right side of your face.

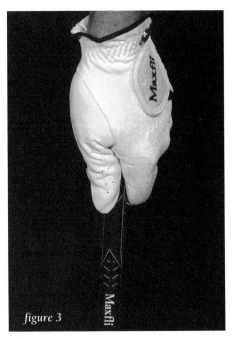

figure 3

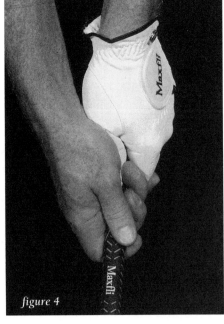

figure 4

A Hacker No More

- The left thumb is at "one o'clock" and the right thumb is at "eleven o'clock."

- The palms of your hands should face each other.

- The grip should be light enough so there is no tension in your hands or forearms.

With your new grip take some slow practice swings. Try to get a sense of how it feels throughout the entire swing. Hold the club at the top and practice starting down. Your hands should give you the feeling of gentle control. Place the clubhead first on the ground and raise it straight up and down in front of you with your wrists. You should be able to do this easily. If this motion is jerky then recheck your grip using the four checks given above.

Good Hands

If you have played golf for any amount of time you have probably noticed that your clubs will feel different in your hands from one day to the next. One day your hands will feel soft and supple while other times they will seem stiff and clumsy. The body is constantly going through cycles of change in order to regulate itself, and the feel of your hands is determined by such things as water, blood pressure, sleep, exercise and anxiety. Whatever the reason, the golfer needs a feeling in the hands that is soft and supple.

I often thought that how the club felt in my hands had a direct relationship to "good days" and "bad days" on the golf course. In order to achieve the feeling of having soft hands I developed a little exercise that I use before I leave for the course. I call it the *Spider Drop:*

- Place your hands on a table with your fingers spread and your palms raised from the surface.

- Gently press down on the table so that your fingers spread out.

- Gently raise your hands so that your fingers come together.

- Let your hands hang limp at your sides and shake them. Flex them gently then hold them at your sides and imagine the tension flowing out of the fingertips.

This exercise has helped me attain a soft feeling in my hands and also serves as a reminder of the importance of a light, sensitive grip. The exercise may be of more psychological value than physical, but it does work. I have used it successfully in golf and with pitchers in baseball. The exercise, in preparation to play golf, is a positive indicator of your commitment to improve.

One question that often comes up is whether or not to wear a glove. I wear a glove because it gives me a solid feeling on the club and acts as a means to prevent slippage. Other players say that the glove interferes with the "feel." Basically, it comes down to a matter of personal preference. There are, however, some cautions that you should take. Avoid wearing a glove that is hard and stiff. I keep my gloves in a plastic bag in order to keep them soft and supple. Touring pros change to new gloves about every three holes. Most of us cannot afford this luxury, but I do change gloves after nine holes. On hot, steamy days it is a good idea to make several glove changes because of perspiration. Some players remove their gloves to putt. Again, this is simply a matter of personal choice.

I have noticed that many golfers carry a club between shots. They swing, grip and regrip and, in general, are fidgeting with their hands during the entire round. I would suggest that you put the club in the bag and let your hands relax. By constantly working them you are only creating fatigue and tension. The hands play a vital role in the swing so they must be in good shape during the round.

I will often watch a baseball or football game with a club in my hands. I will grip and regrip, each time running through the four checks for a good grip. This constant practice away from the course helps develop a sense for the correct grip. Eventually, you will be able to tell if you have a correct grip just from feel.

3

SETTING UP FOR SUCCESS

The most critical stage of hitting a golf shot correctly does not occur at the time of the swing itself. The swing, after all, is purely a matter of integrating our motor control to a sense of feel. The twenty to thirty seconds that is often called the pre-shot routine is actually the time that we program ourselves for success or failure. True concentration does not begin when we stand over the ball. The pre-shot routine is a step-by-step procedure of careful calculation and concentration that places all the elements that go into a good golf shot on our side.

See if this sounds familiar. As a poor golfer, I approached a shot by:

- Checking the yardage to the green and selecting the appropriate club

- Taking a practice swing that is much smoother than my actual swing

- Stepping up to the ball, positioning it off of my left heel and checking the target by looking at the green once more

- Firing away

This is the pre-shot routine of about 90 percent of all golfers. The problem is that this pre-shot routine does little to accomplish the essential elements that lead to a good golf shot. The setup should be a careful sequence of mental and physical checks and preparations.

As I researched the pre-shot phase in-depth it became very clear to me that I had vastly underrated its importance. I am sure that if I stopped a high handicapper just before he started to swing and asked the following questions, he would not be able to answer them with any confidence:

What is this shot going to do?

Are you sure of the yardage and your club selection?

Are you perfectly lined up to the target?

Is the ball in the correct position for this shot?

Are there any conditions that are going to affect the shot?

I know that if someone asked me these questions a few years ago, I would begin each answer with "I think ..." Now I can answer each of these questions with "I know ... " The difference is that I now consider this phase as the critical phase. I approached the learning of this phase with three objectives:

- Determine what needs to be done during the pre-shot phase.

- Develop a plan for each thing that has to be done.

- Develop a pre-shot routine that will be simple and effective.

From watching and talking to outstanding golfers I compiled a list of pre-shot preparations and checks that defined what had to be accomplished:

- Shot Strategy
- Course/Lie Considerations
- Club Selection
- Aiming
- Alignment
- Ball Positioning
- Stance

After determining what needed to be done during the pre-shot I researched various techniques for getting each task accomplished. As expected, I found that there were many ways to approach each task. Over a period of time I experimented with a wide assortment of pre-shot tactics and gradually adopted those techniques that produced the best results for my game. I worked on each component separately until I was satisfied that I had reached a level of mastery.

Shot Strategy

Shot strategy deals with the *how* and *where* of the golf shot. Every shot should be planned with the next shot in mind, much as a billiards player is always considering several shots beyond the one he is facing. Many high handicappers hit a ball with only direction in mind. They hit drives in the direction of the middle of the fairway or approach shots in the direction of the green. Shot strategy is the consideration of the exact placement of the shot that will produce the best situation for scoring well on that hole. It also considers the method used to get the ball to that exact spot. Will you loft the ball high so that it stops quickly on the green or will you land it short or run it onto the green? You want to be able to visualize or mentally rehearse the shot so that you have a clear understanding of what you are trying to do.

The key to smart shot strategy is to think ahead. On a par four, for example, I will look at the area around the green and the placement of the pin. I then bring my focus back to the landing area for my drive. I will select an area that will give me the best approach to the pin. Some of the considerations for the determination of the approach might include a second shot that will not have to carry over trouble to the target, or a position that will allow me to hit into an upward slope on the green. In talking to many high handicappers I am always surprised at the number who say they hit a drive in the general direction of the hole and "worry about the second shot when I come to it." A drive straight down the middle is no guarantee of good ball position. If you play on the same course a great deal you should sit down and write out a plan of attack for each hole. Use the plan as a basic guide and adjust for such things as wind, playing conditions and pin placements. As you play your round, keep grabbing peeks at pin placements and green conditions on holes that are in front of you. If possible, observe how balls are reacting as they land on these greens. These little mental notes will go a long way in determining what kind of shot you will hit when you reach them.

The next part of shot strategy is the "how" of the shot. I want to know exactly how the ball will travel to the target. I think it is very important to have a clear idea of what you want the ball to do. In researching this aspect of the game, I found that almost all good golfers visualize the upcoming shot as a rehearsal. In their minds they "see" the shot fly through the air and land at a designated spot. On the other hand, I found that high handicappers never visualize the shot and remain at the wishing and hoping level. As I developed my game through practice I also developed the ability to visualize. By hitting hundreds of 7-iron shots in practice, I was able to develop a mental picture of what a good 7-iron shot looked like if I had hit it correctly. Visualization is not picturing a 300-yard drive down the middle but it is a realistic reflection of the kind of shot that matches your capability.

As I step up to a typical 7-iron shot I visualize a nice smooth swing and a descending blow that hits down and through the ball; the ball rises then falls softly to the green, bounces and settles down quietly. Visualization is not just wishful thinking. It helps determine club selection, evaluates the type of shot needed and creates confidence by matching ability to expectation. Later on we will discuss techniques for developing your visualization ability.

The key is to select a shot that gets the job done best. Do I hit a high shot that lands softly or do I run it on? Know what you are going to do with the ball on every shot.

Course/Lie Conditions

Understanding the effects of course and lie conditions is simply a matter of experience and judgement. Wind, wetness, texture of the greens, trouble spots and how the ball lies on the ground can all have a substantial impact on the quality of the golf shot you play. An approach shot to a hard, fast green is an entirely different shot than one into a soft, wet one. The ability to read conditions and adjust properly is a necessary characteristic of a good golfer's makeup.

During the pre-shot it is imperative to keep the playing conditions and the effects of various lies in mind. This is just one more way in which the smart golfer stacks the deck for a good shot. Experience is the best teacher when it comes to learning how conditions affect a golf shot. Most golfers develop a sense of how conditions impact on the shot in a relatively short time but fail to make the necessary adjustments during actual play. For example, if the course is wet, I know that the ball will fly with a minimum of backspin, that greens will hold better and that putts will not break as much as under dry conditions. A ball sitting on top of the grass will fly higher and farther than normal, while a ball sitting down in the grass will fly on a low plane. A ball on a downhill lie needs to be played back in the stance and struck in a downward motion. The key is to recognize what factors are coming into play for the shot based on the environment. We will discuss specific techniques for various trouble shots later in the book.

One condition that seems to cause the high handicapper the most problems is the wind. I have often seen golfers test for wind by using two methods. They take a pinch of grass, toss it in the air and watch to see how it falls, or they simply look to see how the flag is blowing. When you think about it both of these techniques may be inadequate for determining how the wind will affect your shot. The wind will have its greatest impact on the ball when the shot reaches the peak of its flight and begins to descend. The wind at your shoulder's height has little effect because the ball is traveling at its highest velocity at impact. The ball descending near the pin has already traveled 99 percent of its flight. To obtain the best indication of wind effect look at the tops of the trees near where your ball will hit its peak. Make your adjustments based on the strength of the wind at that level. If there are no trees look for dust, leaves or birds as indicators of high-level winds.

Club Selection

Selecting the right tool to do the job is critical to the golf shot. Too often, high handicappers rely on yardage alone as the sole criterion for selecting a club. As I looked specifically at this component I found a need to eliminate guesswork and develop a way of consistently putting the correct club into my hands.

Almost every golf instruction book has an obligatory chart equating clubs and distance. We are told that a 7-iron should produce a shot of 150 yards. This equation does not make much sense for the simple reason that individual differences among golfers may cause a wide range of variance in distance. Even if we have a clear yardage-to-club relationship established in our minds, how do we know we are gauging yardage correctly? The method that I have adopted to my game does away with charts and the guessing involved with yardage. The easiest and most effective way of selecting the proper amount of club is to "walk myself" to the target. I start by looking along the target line from the ball to the target. I mentally picture how far a 9-iron would take me toward the target and then "walk" myself up through the clubs until I come to the one that brings me to the target. I usually say to myself, "I can hit a 9-iron that far ... an 8-iron will bring me there ... a 7-iron will ... " and so on. This method of club selection is based on how far you hit each iron. Each visualized shot takes into consideration such things as wind and wetness. As you practice you will gain a better understanding of how far you can hit each club.

Aim and Alignment

Aiming along with its counterpart, alignment, is a real nemesis for the struggling golfer. Most golfers think that they are aiming correctly—when in fact, they are significantly steering themselves off-line. The shot is doomed before the swing is made. The need is to simplify the aiming process so that an accurate target line is developed every time.

Aiming at a target and setting our bodies in proper alignment to the target line are more difficult than normally perceived. Most high handicappers align themselves with their feet while sighting in on a distant target. This procedure just does not get the job done because it is a simple attempt at a complex task. Aiming and alignment have to be approached from a sound technique and a well-thought-out standpoint.

While aiming and alignment are two distinct concepts, they must go hand in hand in setting up for a golf shot. Several years ago I would aim and align much in the same manner as 90 percent of all golfers. I would step up to the hole, look at the pin then set my feet according to the line at which I was looking. The problem with this method is that too many things are overlooked. First of all, by standing up to the ball and looking at the pin, all we are learning is that our eyes can make a straight line from our head to the pin. Remember, the target line is from the ball to the pin or target. Secondly, it would take an extraordinary sense of direction to place our feet in an accurate line to a pinpoint target that is 175 yards away. A surveyor will tell you how difficult that feat is.

The method that I use now is used by many touring pros and is found in many other sports as well. The beauty is in its simplicity.

Start by getting directly behind your ball and sighting down the line created between your ball and the target. Now, bring your eyes back down the target line and find a spot about three feet in front of your ball along the line. The spot can be a divot, pebble, burned-out area, patch of discolored grass

figure 5

or anything that will mark the target line (*see figure 5*). Pro bowlers very rarely look at the pins during delivery. They look at the spots that are marked on the alleys and roll the ball for the spot. A marksman aligns the rear sight of a rifle to the front sight along the target line in much the same manner.

Once you have the target line set up, all you have to do is align yourself along a line that is three feet long and directly in front of you. (*Note: It is against the rules of golf to place anything in your line as a marker, but you may use anything that is in your line naturally.*)

This one tip has resulted in substantial improvement in my game from the very beginning. I no longer have to use guesswork in lining myself up to the target. I have only had trouble when I looked up at the target and adjusted my alignment. I have grown so confident in this technique that I now have the habit of not looking at the target from the time I find my spot. This habit, I found, is very disconcerting to some of my playing partners as they wonder how I know where I am aiming. However, it may be a good idea to look up once before you hit for the sake of comfort. The key is to trust your three-foot target line and not move your address position to suit your eyes.

Setting Up for Success

figure 6

A Hacker No More

To align yourself along the target line you must imagine three lines running parallel to the target line. The three lines are created by 1) feet, 2) hips and 3) shoulders (*see figure 6*). Your swing plane or path of the club will be dictated by the position of your hips and shoulders at impact. Setting your feet square to the line by themselves is not enough to overcome the problem of misaligned hips and shoulders. I have noticed many golfers, plagued by slicing, try to correct their fault by changing foot position. The real culprits, in many of these cases, are the hips and shoulders. I have observed another common problem in the player who opens his hips and shoulders then closes the face of the club to compensate. This is only making the game harder than it already is. I simply say to myself, "Shoulders, hips, feet and clubface—square to the spot."

Ball Positioning

Where should the ball be placed in the stance for this particular shot? How far from the ball should I stand? What do I look at when I swing? These are the questions that must be answered in order to produce consistent shots. High handicappers seem to disregard ball position as an important component of the game. Bad ball positioning is probably the number one cause of inconsistent results.

There are two schools of thought on where the ball should be placed in your stance during the setup. Some experts feel that all shots should be played off of the left heel with the stance becoming narrower as the club length grows shorter. Others propose that the ball should be placed off of the left heel for the driver then moved back toward the right foot as the clubs grow shorter.

For several years I played all of my shots off of the left heel with the rationale that it would simplify things and promote consistency. In taking a careful look at my game, I realized that many of my bad shots took the form of topped or fat hits. Topped and fat shots are red-flag warnings of poor ball positioning. Reduced to the bottom line, it is a matter of the clubhead reaching the impact position before the ball is struck properly. It just does not seem logical to me that the ball should remain in the same position while the lengths of the clubs differ. As I thought about this, I came to the conclusion that the truly superior golfers are able to use this method because of their superior talent. The adjustments required are within their capabilities but are beyond the scope of most of the rest of us.

I decided to switch to the more conventional approach of changing the position of the ball according to the club length. To set the proper position for each club I used the following technique to calibrate each setting:

- Take a normal swing with a 5-iron, paying attention to maintain good rhythm and tempo.
- Mark the spot where the club touches the ground.
- This spot is the position for your 5-iron. For each longer club move the ball one half-ball width toward your left foot. For each shorter club move the ball one half-width toward your right foot. The driver should be off of your left instep while the wedge will be just inside the right.
- Let comfort be your guide in making subtle adjustments. Avoid extremes and any position that causes you to make severe changes in your swing plane.
- Once you establish your ball position settings, stick with them and practice consistently using the positions.

One often-overlooked aspect of ball position that is the source of many problems is the distance that one should stand from the ball. There is an old joke about the guy who says that his problem is that he stands too close to the ball—after he hits it. As I see it, most poor golfers seem to stand too far from the ball at address. Take a look at the address positions of many golfers at a driving range or on the first tee on a Sunday morning. Many of them extend both arms fully to the ball, bend severely from the waist or get themselves in a crouch position by bending their knees and "sitting down." These setup positions usually produce a flat swing. Flat swings are characterized by low hand position at the top of the swing as opposed to having the hands high and upright. The flat swing usually results in a loss of distance and accuracy.

In order to gauge the proper distance that you should stand from the ball, try the following method:

- Take a normal stance with a slight bend at your waist and a slight flex in your knees.
- Lay the club down so that the grip end lies between your feet.
- Now, position your feet so that the point where the grip meets the shaft is aligned with your instep.
- The clubhead will lie at the point where you should place the ball.

If this position looks very close to you, chances are you have been standing too far away from the ball—before you hit it! By moving closer to the ball I naturally developed a more upright swing plane. Additionally, I gained a better balance. In the past, I would often finish my swing with the feeling that my weight was on my toes. By moving closer, my balance has shifted to the insides of my feet.

A Hacker No More

Taking a Stance

The proper stance dictates the amount of balance and type of swing plane that we make. By standing correctly and adjusting the stance to accommodate the shot, we program ourselves for proper swing mechanics. The stance is not something that we automatically develop through practice. It is a component of the pre-shot routine that needs to be checked with every shot.

The placement of the feet serves two purposes in golf—alignment and balance. The width between the feet directly affects your ability to make a proper turn during the swing. To test this relationship, stand with your feet about three inches outside of each shoulder and take a normal swing. You will notice that your ability to make a full turn with your hips and shoulder is severely restricted. While most of us would never consider using a stance this wide, the average golfer does take one that is too wide to be effective. Many of us who grew up playing baseball are accustomed to the wide stance that gave us leverage when swinging the bat. The baseball swing with a bat is a horizontal plane that requires much different leg movements from that of the golf swing. A wide stance in golf is often and erroneously associated with leverage.

Weight transfer, shoulder- and hip-turn along with the downward thrust to impact all dictate that the stance should be about shoulder-width while hitting the driver. As the clubs decrease in length the width of the feet becomes narrower. The back foot should be almost perpendicular to your target line. This is the foot that kicks into the ball. During the downswing you will push off of this foot toward the target. If your back foot is turned away from the target line your power will be misdirected. The left or front foot should be opened or turned slightly toward the target. This open position allows for a proper pivot and prevents swaying. As the club length is decreased, the left foot should be opened increasingly with each club. This adjustment is needed to accommodate the shorter, tighter backswing with the shorter clubs.

One thing that I have noticed about high handicappers' stances is that they are very inconsistent. I have played with golfers who set up a drive with a wide stance on one tee and then a narrow one on the next. As you practice, make it a point to check the width of your stance with each swing until you develop consistency. By constantly changing your width you are creating disruptive forces in your sense of balance. You will not notice the loss of balance until you have started your swing. Check your feet first!

At the address position you should flex your knees slightly, bend from the waist with your back straight and position your shoulders so that the left is slightly higher than the right (*see figures 7 and 8*). Your feet, hips and

figure 7

A Hacker No More

figure 8

shoulders should all point straight down the target line. The address position should feature a left side that creates a straight line from your left shoulder to the clubhead. The hands are slightly ahead of the ball and your weight is centered on the insides of your feet. The address position should be completely free of tension. As a test, many teaching professionals ask that their students hold the address position for 90 seconds. If shaking or tension develop during that time frame then there is tension present at the outset. You should feel loose and fluid over the ball, ready to make a smooth, well-timed swing.

Pre-shot Routine

Consistency breeds consistency. Once you have mastered the principles involved in the pre-shot, you need to develop a routine that will ensure that you execute each component correctly each and every time that you step up to the ball. The good golfer uses the pre-shot phase to stack the deck in his or her favor by ensuring that all the components have been checked and executed.

As you read through the list of things that need to be done during the pre-shot phase you probably thought it would take ten minutes to accomplish. Actually, everything can be effectively carried out in a thirty second time frame. I use a set routine every time in order to accomplish these tasks:

- As I am walking up to my ball I am formulating my shot strategy. I decide on the *where* and the *how* of the shot first. I also determine the course conditions, particularly wind and wetness.

- I step up to the ball and check the lie, feel the ground under my feet and run through my club selection process by "walking myself" to the target.

- I step behind the ball, get my target line and find my three-foot marking spot.

- I move over the ball, then align my clubhead, feet, hips and shoulders along the target line and check my stance.

- From a relaxed address position I begin my backswing with a feeling that I have done everything possible to set myself up for a good shot. I now try to drive the ball over my three-foot spot.

These steps do not need to be rushed. Go through this routine in practice with every shot that you hit. You will develop a systematic way of setting up for success every time.

4

THE BEST SWING POSSIBLE

Ben Hogan once said, "Golf cannot be taught, only learned." In order to totally remake my game, I realized that I had to be a total learner. I needed to learn everything I could about the good golf swing: what it looked like and, more importantly, what it felt like. Once I set out to learn the swing from scratch I decided to approach it from a sound educational perspective. I did not rush out to the practice tee; rather, I sat down and sketched out a blueprint of just how I would accomplish my goal. My professional life centered on learning. It made sense to utilize my experience and training to learn how to develop a good golf swing.

In making an honest appraisal of my golf swing, I realized that no quick cure, such as a grip change alone, would produce significant improvement. I decided to build a great swing from scratch rather than to modify my old one. If I were playing near-par golf, a few modifications may have been appropriate, but I was not a good golfer, and all I had going for me was a burning desire to become one.

The very first thing that I did was to write out my goal.

Goal: A smooth, solid swing that yields satisfying and consistent results.

Now, you might think that this is a strange thing to write as a goal, but just think about it for a minute. Take a look at the golfers on a crowded practice tee or driving range. Ninety percent of them are smacking balls down-range in machine-gun fashion while using the same swing over and over. How many of them have you seen pause to check their grip, stance, alignment, posture and swing plane? In golf, practice does not necessarily make perfect; nor does quantity mean quality.

By writing out my goal I set forth a purpose for everything I did in order to learn the game. Every time I picked up a club to practice, read an instruction book, watched a video or visited a PGA Tour event, I had my one goal in mind. I resolved, for example, never to hit a ball in practice without concentrating on making the best swing possible. I think that this point deserves careful consideration as it is the demarcation line between the average golfer and the top player. Most golfers experience significant improvement for the first two to three years after they take up the game. They improve to a point, then hit a plateau that they stay at for the rest of their golf lives. Take a look at the handicap board at your club and compare it to five years ago. You will find that the vast majority of members are still hovering within two strokes either way of their old handicap. To really learn the game and make major improvements you have to have a clear idea of where you want to go and a plan of how to get there.

Taking an Inventory

After stating my goal, my next step was to take an inventory of my golf swing to establish just where I was. In education, teachers will always give a pretest to establish a starting point before introducing new material. A research scientist will measure such things as temperature and density of a substance before an experiment in order to establish baseline data. In the golf swing we need to find out how our swings differ from what is proper. Since the golf swing is a matter of feel, I wanted to know what things I was doing correctly and how I felt at each point. I also wanted to know the base-line data on the parts that needed major change.

In order to take an inventory I decided to compare my tempo and various survey positions to those of the very best swings. I sifted through stacks of old golf magazines and pulled out all the detailed, stop-action photos of the pros' swings that I could find. I settled on one particular set (Gene Littler's) as my model. Modeling is a sound educational practice that I have used in the classroom and on the playing field as a coach.

I bought a cheap, full-length mirror from a discount department store and set it up on the side of my garage. I studied the stop-action photos, then assumed my positions in front of the mirror. I would study my address position, then Gene's; my takeaway, then his. I would go through every part of the swing inch by inch and make comparisons with the model swing. Self-perception is often deceiving. What we think is a high, strong position at the top of our swings may indeed be a flat, awkward one. If you have access to a video or a Polaroid camera, so much the better. The idea is to gain an appreciation of where you are in the swing in order to establish a learning base. If you realize that your position at the top is poor, you will know that the proper position will require a different feel and time for adjustment while learning is taking place.

Building a Knowledge Base

As I said earlier, I knew a good golf swing when I saw one. I needed to know the why and how of the mechanics required to produce an effective swing. Once I knew the how and why of the swing movements I would be able to work on incorporating them into a swing of my own and learn how the swing felt. I realized that the knowledge of the swing in itself would not transform me into a good golfer. It was, however, a starting point from which to grow.

I listened to pros, good amateur players and poor golfers alike. As I spoke to these golfers I tried to compare and contrast the ideas that I heard. I felt that it was important to understand how the high handicapper approached the development of the swing in order to gain a perspective on what separates the top golfers from those who struggle on the course. To my surprise, many high handicappers had a sound foundation in the fundamentals of the golf swing. Often, I would hear something like, "I know what to do; I just can't do it."

I spent a great deal of time watching golf videos. I would often play and replay the swings of the pros over and over and make notes on particular observations of swing technique. The video is an advantageous learning tool for a couple of reasons: 1) it gives you a sense of rhythm and tempo and 2) it creates a visual memory of the proper swing that serves as an instructional model and also serves as a basis for visualization during the pre-shot.

The one area of building my knowledge base that had the most pronounced impact on me was watching the pros up close at a PGA Tour event. I have been to many tour events in the past and at one time served as a marshal at the Tournament of Champions at La Costa. However, in the past I went to these events as a spectator and watched the pros as I would watch a quarterback at a football game. I marveled at their swings and was in awe of their skills. It was simply a day of enjoyment.

As an active learner, however, I went to the PGA events with a completely different agenda. I would study every aspect of the great players' games like a clinician. At one event, the Bank of Boston Classic at Pleasant Valley, I spent over eight hours in observation, yet I only spent about one hour on the course itself. The rest of the time was spent in the laboratory—the practice tee. On the practice tee I had the opportunity to study the great swings up close. I was able to study swing technique in depth and gain insight into the practice routine itself. Beyond the swing, I was struck by the level of concentration and the careful attention to detail that I observed with each shot. As I studied the players I remarked to myself that there was something very different here. That something was not the great shots flying down-range but the precise, surgeon-like manner in which the best golfers hit the golf ball.

I made my observations by breaking down the swing into components for study. I would spend a half-hour watching the setup; then I would spend a half-hour observing how the takeaway was made. I would move my eyes from one pro to the next to focus on the one aspect that I had chosen to observe. I moved to various positions around the tee in order to get different perspectives. On the course I concerned myself with such things as pre-shot routine, strategy and special shots (sand, rough, lob). I came away from that tournament with a clear idea of what it takes to become a good golfer. My next step was to put my knowledge into an action plan to build the best swing possible. I started a step-by-step approach to building the skills required to make the correct movements at every phase of the swing. I began with the backswing.

Taking the Club Back

The purpose of the backswing is twofold. One, it is a means of getting the club into a position to start the club toward impact. Two, it creates an arc that serves as a guide for the downswing. The takeaway and backswing are more important to the golf swing than most realize. The success of a shot may well be determined by the first few movements back.

Before we discuss the mechanics of the backswing, I think it is very important to address the element of club speed during the backswing. The concepts of rhythm and tempo are often used to describe how the speed of the swing should be studied. Rhythm describes the proper flow of body movements during the swing. For example, the downswing should start with a sliding of the hips toward the target. Starting the downswing with your hands is an example of falling out of rhythm. Tempo is an important element of rhythm. It refers to the speed of the body movements during the swing. A tempo that is too fast or too slow will disrupt the natural flow of the swing.

Most backswing instruction cautions us against becoming too fast. Every time you hit a bad shot, it seems that a playing partner tells you to "slow it down." Yet as I studied how poor golfers swing, it was very obvious that most of them had slow backswings. On the other hand, I was surprised at the backswing speed of the touring pros. Looking at my own swing, I realized that my extra-slow backswing was a source of disruption for my rhythm and tempo.

I would very slowly move the club back to about the halfway point of the backswing. Then I would make a jerky, lifting motion with my hands to get the club to the position at the top. It was simply a matter of physics. Because I took the club back so slowly, I needed to tense and make a lifting motion to get the club all the way back. This movement, although subtle, would send the club off my intended arc and cause a wide assortment of problems. As I watched high handicappers play, I realized that an overly slow backswing is far more prevalent than one that is too fast.

I was fascinated by the tempo and rhythm of the touring pros' backswings. They could not be described as fast or slow. Rather, they seemed to make a smooth, deliberate sweep at a moderate speed. The speed of the touring pros' backswings was quite a bit faster than I had expected, but it was clear that they maintained command and control of the club throughout this movement. When you practice the backswing, I think it is beneficial to keep your swing-thought one of making a *smooth sweep to the top*. The speed should be sufficient to move the clubhead to the top position without having to make any lifting motions with your hands or arms. A light grip combined with a *smooth sweep* is the key for taking the club back with proper speed.

To learn the backswing I used the picture and mirror method. This technique produces excellent results because, by getting into the proper position and checking it for accuracy, you are accomplishing two important things for learning:

- You gain an appreciation of what the proper position feels like.

- You begin to train your muscles to produce the movements to get you into the position.

Rather than begin with the takeaway, as most backswing instruction does, I think it is more important to see where you are going with the takeaway. If you have a clear idea of what position you need to get to, you will be able to develop a better idea of how to get there. With all the twists and turns that have to be orchestrated, the backswing can be made very complicated. I decided to make it as simple as possible and used the concept of *hitting my spots* to create a good backswing.

The *spots* are like stop-action photos at a particular point in the swing. I decided on hitting these spots as checkpoints to ensure that my swing was on track. For the backswing, I selected two spots. The first spot is halfway into the backswing, and the second comes at the position at the top. It is important to stress that these are not stopping points—*they are learning techniques that occur as momentary points of a smooth movement.*

The Two Spots

The first spot occurs at the point where your left arm is fully extended backward and where the hands begin to start upward—just below halfway into your backswing. In this position the left shoulder is turned slightly toward your chin, and your left knee is flexed inward while your right knee begins to straighten. Your weight begins to shift to the right side. There is no feeling of stiffness or strain. Your left arm is straight but not stiff.

Now try to assume the position. If you feel more comfortable making a slight swinging motion to get to this position, then fine—do it. Now check yourself in the mirror and make adjustments. Look at your feet, knees, hips, arms, hands, shoulders and head. If you have had serious flaws in your swing, it may take a while before you can make the proper adjustments comfortably. Keep your grip light and avoid tensing any muscles. As a drill, keep taking the position or spot over and over each time, checking it in the mirror. Try to feel the clubhead in your hands. Get a sense of exactly what it feels like to be in this position. Commit this feeling to memory with repeated practice and check in front of the mirror. Make it part of you.

The second spot is the position at the top of the swing (see figure 9). The shoulders are turned ninety degrees, with the left shoulder placed just left of your chin. The left arm is fully extended (not stiff), with the left forearm, wrist and hand forming a straight line. The right elbow is flexed and points downward at an angle. The left foot has rolled toward your right, and the left heel is slightly lifted from the ground. The left knee is pointing inward, and the right leg is straightened to support your weight.

To assume this position, it is best to make a swinging motion up to the spot. If you have mastered the first spot, you might start there and gently move up to the top. You need not hold this position for any length of time to learn it, but you should check your position in the mirror. Check every aspect of your position, starting with your feet and moving up. The hips should turn naturally, as a result of leg and shoulder movement. One thing that should be emphasized in this position is to get your hands high. Get the feeling that you are throwing them over your head as high as possible. At this point, your hands are in a position that holds the club firmly and extends the club parallel to the ground. Keep drilling yourself to perfect your position. I spent many hours learning these spots, so allow yourself the time to master them.

Learning how these positions look and feel, you should develop a mental picture and muscle memory of these two checkpoints. I don't worry about forty-five-degree pronation, supination of the wrists or thirty-degree hip-turn and so forth. I know what the correct positions look and feel like during the backswing, and I simply concentrate on hitting my spots. Ballet dancers, who have to make movements that are more precise and demanding than the golf swing, will train in much the same manner as I have described. Dance studios are usually walled with mirrors for the dancers to check their positions as they develop muscle memory of the required positions.

The positions will become second nature to you through practice. It is important to do your drills over and over in order to master them. It is at these stages of learning that you must make up your mind to train your psychomotor domain to perform correctly. Remember, you are learning new concepts and movements and eradicating bad habits that have been developed over your golfing lifetime. It will take time and persistence, but there are great days of golf ahead of you as your reward.

figure 9

A Hacker No More

The Takeaway

To start the clubhead back, many good players use some form of a forward press or waggle to break the moment of inertia. The idea behind this movement is to prevent the hands lagging behind the club, or worse, moving the clubhead back in a sharp, jerky motion. I tried several different movements before I settled on one that seemed comfortable and practical. Some players move their hands forward slightly, then start the club back. This movement may actually total about one inch. Others make a shifting movement with their feet, shuffling from one foot to the other. One movement that you see quite often in the poor golfer's takeaway is a series of "false starts," where the player starts back and forth several times before he launches into a real takeaway. To me, this only serves to promote too much wrist action and hand tension.

I decided to firm my grip slightly and straighten my left arm just before I start the club back. I do not move my feet, head, shoulders or hands; my aim is to keep everything as simple as possible. The less things move, the less things can go wrong.

As I step up to the ball, I have the club in a light, feathery grip. I waggle it back and forth a few times to gain a feel for the clubhead. Throughout the swing, you should have a sense of swinging the clubhead instead of manipulating the grip and shaft. I settle into a position that has my weight on the insides of my feet, with a feeling that I am perfectly balanced, standing fairly upright and completely free of tension. With a clear idea of my target line, I make the slight firming motion with my hands and start the club back straight along the target line. I think that it is very important to gain a sense of taking the club back straight, as it establishes the proper swing path for the club.

Some of the worst advice I have ever received involves the takeaway. Many people promote the idea that you should take the club back to the inside in order to create an inside-out swing plane. I have seen many golfers take this advice to heart and pull the club back just beyond their right foot. This is simply a bad idea and bad advice. As you make your takeaway, take the club back along the target line as far back as possible. Your normal shoulder- and hip-turn will bring the club to the inside. Golf teachers seem compelled to tell us that it is impossible to take the club back straight. Of course, it is impossible to keep the club in a straight line back from the ball throughout the backswing, but the club should start back straight and stay as near to the target line for as long as possible. The longer the club is along the target line, both in the takeaway and through impact, the better chance there is for a solid, straight shot. If you pull the club sharply to the inside of the target line at takeaway, you will probably have to make a corrective move later in your backswing. Often, this corrective move takes form as a loop at the top of the swing in which the club gets thrown outside the target line and results in a slice.

All through my practice routines and into actual play, I use what are called swing cues. Swing cues are little phrases or reminders that serve to promote concentration on certain movements. For example, when I practice the backswing, I will say to myself, "sweep." The word reminds me to get a feeling of sweeping the clubhead back and through my spots.

While practicing the takeaway itself, I will often use the swing cue, "low and slow." This cue prompts me to start the club back smoothly, without any attempt to pick it up as I start back. The clubhead should not start upward until the left arm is fully extended backward (*see figure 10*). There is no conscious effort to lift the club up. The movement is a natural sweep to the top that is free of any attempts to manipulate the club with your hands or arms.

The purpose of the backswing is to get yourself into a proper position at the top. It is actually a coiling movement that precedes the uncoiling which delivers a descending blow down and through the ball. The high handicapper tends to have a backswing that is controlled mostly by the hands and arms. The backswing is actually a combination of turns involving the hands, arms, feet, hips and shoulders. To learn the proper turning movements, I broke down the backswing into sub-skills and created drills that develop mastery.

Shoulders. The shoulders should make a ninety-degree turn back to impact. In order to learn this movement, I used the swing cue, "left shoulder under, right shoulder under." This cue tells me to bring my left shoulder almost under my chin as I reach the position at the top of the swing and to place my right shoulder under my chin just after impact. In addition to drilling the technique of making a full and correct shoulder-turn, this exercise also helps you keep your head anchored as the hub of your turn. If you cannot bring your shoulders almost under your chin at the top position and just after impact, it means that you are probably swaying or moving your head. Start using this drill very slowly to gain a feel for it. Check yourself in the mirror to make sure that, as your shoulder comes just to the left of your chin, your arms are extended fully to the top of your swing. By practicing this movement in slow motion, you may also set up your timing and tempo. When you turn so that your shoulder is almost under your chin, you will know that you have just about completed your backswing and are now ready to start down. In a way, you are taking the guesswork out of when to finish the backswing and when to start the downswing.

Feet. Proper foot action is essential to the good swing, and the key is moderation. Too little footwork restricts turning and promotes a stiff arm and hand swing. A lack of proper footwork also causes swaying. Too much foot

figure 10

action throws the club off the proper swing plane and destroys tempo. The key to proper foot action is to keep your weight on the insides of your feet during the swing. If, for example, you find that your weight seems to fall on the outside of your right foot during the backswing, you are probably swaying as a result of too much footwork. The inside-balance "feel" should be kept right through impact, when your weight shifts almost entirely to your left side. With the longer clubs the left heel rises slightly from the ground at the top of the swing. This heel rise should decrease as the clubs grow shorter, until there is almost no lift with the pitching wedge.

In order to learn proper footwork, I used the following drill. I would take a normal stance of about shoulder width, with my left foot slightly open and my right foot perpendicular to the target line. I take a normal upright stance and place my hands in front of me with palms open, right hand on top of the left hand. I place a mirror so that my entire focus is on my feet. Without a club, I do not have to be concerned about anything except footwork. I swing my hands back to simulate a backswing and downswing, while I concentrate on making a weight shift that stays to the insides of my feet. I concentrate on keeping my balance centered in the middle of my body. I simply swing back and forth, checking my foot action in the mirror and concentrating on keeping my balance centered. I repeat this drill over and over in order to train my feet to keep that balanced feeling throughout the swing.

Legs. Because the legs are the source of power in the swing, they must coil back so that they can generate this power on the downswing. When I set up, I feel that my knees are pointed slightly inward as a result of having my weight on the insides of my feet. Again, there is no tension in the legs, but a comfortable feeling of being slightly flexed at the knees. During the backswing, the left knee kicks in toward the center as the left heel rises slightly. The right leg straightens to support the weight shift, but there is no stiffness and the right knee does not lock (*see figure 11*). As a drill, I use the same technique as with footwork. Swing back and forth without a club, concentrating on maintaining balance and developing a feel of coiling back.

Hips. In the address position, the hips should line up straight along the target line. The hips turn back in concert with the feet, legs and shoulders during the backswing. This point became very obvious to me when I tried to develop a hip-turn. I was once told that I made no turn with my hips. As I tried to turn them during the swing, I found myself making jerky movements that threw my tempo off completely. The pelvic and hip muscles are not a group of muscles that readily respond to independent drill. But with proper footwork and shoulder-turns, your hips should make a natural turn. Check to see that your hips turn back and forth as you work on your feet and shoulder drills.

figure 11

Hands and Wrists. The advanced golfer and the hacker differ significantly in the use of hands and wrists during the backswing. When the good golfer takes care of the feet and shoulder fundamentals while sweeping the club back to the position at the top, the hands and wrists take care of themselves, making a natural roll during the movement to the top. On the other hand, the high handicapper tries to manipulate the club through hand and wrist movements that can cause the club to move off of a set swing plane.

During the takeaway, you should have a feeling of starting back in "one piece." The hands, arms and shoulders all turn back, with no wrist movement, to lift or control the club. Think of a straight line drawn from your left shoulder all the way down to the clubhead. As you start back, this entire line moves back without any breaks. The wrists remain in the same position as they had in the address. As you make your turn back and hit your first spot, your wrists will make a natural roll that opens the clubface. As you move through the first spot, your wrists will begin to cock until you reach your position at the top. This gradual cocking motion is the reason why you must have a good feel for the clubhead instead of trying to control the club with your hands. It is the clubhead that causes your wrists to roll and cock, not a conscious effort on your part. If you make a sweeping motion back with your left arm fully extended, there is no reason to worry about what your hands and wrists are doing. Concentrate on hitting your spots as a drill, and the hands and wrists will take care of themselves.

Looking at the Ball. One question that often comes up is how to look at the ball during the address and swing. This concept is important as the golf swing is the result of a good eye-muscle relationship. As an instructor in the Marine Corps, I learned the master-eye technique, a method of shooting quickly and accurately in emergencies by focusing your master eye on a line between the tip of the rifle and your target. The master eye is the eye that pinpoints a target. If you are right-handed, chances are your right eye is your master eye. To find your master eye, point at a distant object with both eyes opened. Close one eye and then the other. The eye that brings your finger onto the target is your master eye. In golf, you should position your head so that your master eye has a clear shot at the ball.

One very good golfer told me that he focuses on one dimple where the club should come in contact with the ball. I found that the concentration required to do this caused too much tension and was too difficult for me to maintain during the swing. I tend to look at the back half of the ball throughout the swing. I find this method to be both comfortable and manageable. Some players use little tricks on the tee, such as lining up the brand name of the ball along the target line or placing the ball number at the point of impact. The key is to find a comfortable position that enables you to hold your focus on the ball throughout the swing. If you find that you have difficulty maintaining a good picture of the ball throughout the swing, you may be moving your head too much.

When I set out to practice the backswing, I use the following checkpoints each time:

- Start the club back along the target line after a slight movement to break inertia.

- Sweep back straight with the swing thought, "low and slow."

- Left arm and hand extend straight backward as you hit the first spot

- Legs, hips and shoulders all turn in unison—no jerky movements

- Hands are nice and high at the second spot. Left arm fully extended but not stiff

The Downswing

If I had to select the one critical point in the swing that distinguishes the good golfer from the poor golfer, it would be the point where the downswing starts. It is at the top of the swing that the high handicapper does such things as letting go with his wrists (casting), looping or simply the hands reverting to a hand-and-arm swing. Special care and attention must be given to the first movements of the downswing or the whole swing will be thrown off-plane.

Before you can start your downswing, you must finish the backswing. You must have a solid mental and physical cue for when you have reached the proper position at the top of the swing. This is why I began with the spot method. Once you have mastered your spot at the top, you will automatically know that your shoulders are turned ninety degrees, with your left shoulder under your chin, your left arm fully extended and your hands high (*see figure 12*). You have a feeling of being coiled in your feet and legs and that you are ready to strike down. Once you hit your spot, a little signal should tell you that all systems are go for the downswing. Often, you will hear someone say, "I rushed it" after a bad shot. Usually, he has not moved too quickly but started the downswing before reaching the top of the swing position.

You should never consciously pause at the top of the swing. Old instruction books talk about a pause because old whippy shaft clubs required a pause to allow the clubhead to come back. But a pause at the top only breaks the natural rhythm of the swing. Let your mind cue you when you

figure 12

A Hacker No More

have reached your spot and when to start back. Some good players practice with a count such as "one … and … two," with the "and" a timing signal to start down between the "one" of the backswing and the "two" of the downswing.

There is wide debate about which action starts the clubhead down, but most good players believe it centers in the legs and feet. My first movement in the downswing is a shifting feeling in which my left heel returns to the ground as it receives the shift in weight, my left knee slides back toward the left, and my hips slide laterally toward the target. The movement of my hips is not a turn but a slide that sets up position for uncoiling. These first few, subtle movements start the momentum toward the ball and transfer motion upwards toward my shoulders. As my feet, legs and hips all move toward the left, my shoulders must start to uncoil toward the left and begin to pull my arms and hands.

During the swing, my shoulders act as the spokes around a hub. My left arm remains straight (not stiff) and my wrists cock as my left shoulder moves toward the target and starts to pull up slightly. The key feeling at this point is that I am pulling down with my hands and arms. Many professionals describe this feeling as "pulling the chain." If you placed your hands on a chain or rope to simulate the position at which you start your downswing and pulled straight down, you would feel the same sensation of pulling into the downswing. The pulling down movement is important for three reasons:

- It creates a steadily increasing thrust caused by the movement of the legs and shoulders.

- It delays the uncocking of the wrists.

- It holds the clubhead in the correct swing plane.

The gradual increase in thrust toward the ball is caused by the shoulders turning and pulling the arms and hands along for the ride. There should be no feeling of exertion of muscling the shot at this time. I feel as if I am slowly uncoiling and that my big muscles (back, shoulders) are pulling my arms and hands in a slinging manner.

By using the turning motion of my shoulders to key my swing movements, I can eliminate my hands and arms from going off on their own and throwing the club off of the proper swing plane. The "left shoulder under, right shoulder under" swing cue is all I need to remember to turn properly and stay in control of the swing.

I get the feeling of "pulling the chain" by holding my wrists in the cocked position and keeping my left arm fully extended into the downswing. The turning of my shoulders causes the arms and hands to move at increased speed toward impact, but my main concern is to hold my arms and wrists in the cocked position for as long as possible.

Impact

As I come into the ball, I feel that my shoulders, hips, knees and feet are all driving toward the target. My right foot pushes off while my right knee "kicks" in toward the ball. My balance still remains on the insides of my feet as the weight transfers to my left. I pull down with my arms and hands until my wrists release naturally. My left arm remains straight and leads my hands through impact as they make a natural roll into the hit. I get the feeling that my right hand is snapping the clubhead through the ball as a result of the late release of my wrists. I drive the clubhead down and through the ball at impact and send the clubhead straight down the target line.

In learning the downswing through impact, I used several techniques. For the downswing, I had only one spot. In this position, I am slightly more than halfway toward impact. My left arm is fully extended and my wrists are still cocked (see figure 13). My arm and hand positions are essentially the same as they were in the position at the top. I use this spot as a means to train myself to pull down from the top.

Using a mirror, try to get into this position. Check your feet, hips and shoulders as well as your hands and arms. Once you feel that you can replicate this position, move back to the position at the top or second spot. Practice making a pulling motion from the top of the swing (spot 2) to the halfway point of the downswing (spot 3). Hold your wrists in the cocked position and keep your left arm extended. Turn your shoulders and move your weight to your left side as you move from spot 2 to spot 3. Check yourself in the mirror and against the illustrations to ensure that you are properly executing this important move.

I use many different swing cues, depending on what I want to learn. One swing cue that I use both in practice and when I feel I need a checkup on the course is "sweep-and-pull." During the backswing, I say the word "sweep" very slowly as I move the club back to the position at the top. When I hit the spot at the top of the swing, the "and" serves as the trigger to return my left heel to the ground and to slide my hips toward the target. The word "pull" reminds me to pull into the shot from the top spot right through to the third spot just before release.

figure 13

The Best Swing Possible

Follow-through

As my hands drive through the ball at impact, my hips and shoulders continue to turn and clear out of the way of my arms (*see figure 14*). My weight transfers to the front of my left foot while my right foot rolls and comes up at the heel. I feel that the clubhead is being directed at the target.

While the follow-through in itself does not affect the striking of the ball, it can be used to check balance and swing plane. When I finish, my shoulders and hips are turned slightly left of the target, and my hands are over my left shoulder. If you feel as if you are falling off balance at the end, you may be swaying instead of turning. If your follow-through ends with your clubhead low and in front of you, chances are that you released your wrists from the top (casting) or tried to scoop at the ball with your hands. Try to make a natural and full follow-through. If you find yourself making corrective motions at the end of your follow-through to look proper or to maintain your balance, then you are only covering up some problem in your swing. Remember, the follow-through is a good means of finding out if there is anything wrong in your swing.

Some Thoughts on the Swing

One essential principle of the good golf swing is keeping the head still. The head is the center of our balance. Its movement can severely affect the plane of the swing. By keeping your head still, you anchor yourself in a position that allows you to make a full swing and return to the proper position at impact with consistency. Try to sense that your head is the center of your balance and that your swing goes around that center. Use a mirror to see if you are keeping your head still and to train it to keep still.

Place a string vertically down the middle of the mirror by taping the ends of the string to the top and bottom of the mirror. Now take your address position so that the string cuts through the middle of your head. Make a normal backswing and stop at the position at the top of the swing. Without moving, look up and check to see if you have moved off-center of the string. If you have moved more than one inch, then you will need to practice in front of the mirror to develop a steady head.

One of the most difficult concepts to acquire is tempo. The spot method can help tempo. If you concentrate on hitting your spots, you must get into the correct position at three critical points of the swing. By learning the feel of these spots, your body will continually give you feedback about your timing. If, for example, your hands get to the top of the swing before you have shoulders fully turned, you will immediately become aware of this from feel.

A Hacker No More

figure 14

The Best Swing Possible

Learning the proper swing movements through the use of spots, modeling and mirror-imaging is a method that has been established as a valid training technique in other sports. The Soviet Union has trained its Olympic athletes for years by careful study of movements and mirror-imaging. At the United States Olympic Training Center, computers break down individual performances in frame-by-frame sequences. Specific positions are established where athletes train and check their movements against a norm. This technique is much the same as the one you would use in hitting your spots and checking in the mirror.

A good swing will take hours of hard work on the practice tee. Some things will come faster than others. I made up my mind not to settle for a little improvement. I wanted a great swing and substantial improvement in my scores. Work toward developing the perfect swing and do not think of staying within your capabilities. A good, solid swing can be learned with the proper effort and correct technique. You will be able to measure your improvement in several ways.

Your scores should improve gradually and in proportion to your amount of practice. You will not score better every time that you play, but I like to think you will improve in clusters. As you start out, your scores may cluster around 95 to 105. Ninety-five is a good day, and 105 is a bad day. As you improve, you will move into a new cluster of scores. You might still shoot a 98, but now you are also shooting 88s. Over time, your "good-day-95" will become a "bad-day-95." Keep this in mind as you work toward your goal of becoming a good golfer.

Another way to measure your swing improvement is to simply look at yourself in the mirror, on videotape or on film. You should have gained a good appreciation of what a good golf swing looks like and how yours measures up. I know that I made a complete transformation within two years. Recently, I had an experience that was a tremendous boost to my ego and a little payoff for my many hours of work on the practice tee. I had just driven from a crowded first tee of a public course. I had hit a good drive and moved off to the side of the tee. A guy I had never met came up to me and said, "Excuse me, I didn't see where your drive went, but I just had to tell you—you swing like we all want to." He made my day!

A Hacker No More

5

THE TOOLS OF THE TRADE

No matter what the advertisers tell you, a club that can turn a 70-yard slice into a 220-yard drive down the fairway simply does not exist! Yet, understanding the differences in equipment and how structure, length and "feel" of the club can affect your shot is important to consider.

The Woods

Driver. The driver probably strikes fear into the hearts of high handicappers more than any other club. The most shallow loft and the longest shaft make it a formidable challenge to many players. Too often, however, golfers give up on the driver without giving it a chance. For the good player, the driver is probably second only to the putter in frequency of use. It is a club that can lead to substantial scoring improvement when you learn how to use it properly. The driver belongs in your bag—not in the trunk of your car.

Finding the right driver for you is an important step. To choose the best-fitting driver, seek the guidance of a professional who knows you. When selecting a driver, or any club for that matter, consider the following: shaft, clubhead size, weight, length and feel.

The stiffness of the shaft affects how the clubhead bends or "kicks" in toward the ball at impact. Shafts that are too whippy will give you the feeling of hitting early, without the power generated through hand action. Overly stiff shafts result in late hits and, in turn, in shots or drives that lack distance. For years, I struggled with stiff shafts when I should have been using regular flex ones. There were many factors in my failure to hit the ball straight, but the stiff shafts were not contributing anything positive to my game.

Shafts come in four degrees of stiffness:

- F = Flexible; usually used by women, juniors and elderly players who have a slow, soft downswing

- R = Regulars; moderately stiff flex. The regular shaft probably should be used by about 80 percent of all golfers as it reflects the speed of a normal golf swing

- S = Stiff; the stiff shaft is for the powerful swinger who imparts a great deal of centrifugal force on the clubhead during the downswing

- X = Extra Stiff; extra stiff shafts are for the very, very few power hitters.

The standard length of the driver is about forty-three inches. Short golfers may feel more comfortable using a driver of forty-two, or even forty-one inches, but this choice is mostly a matter of feel. Conversely, tall players

A Hacker No More

need not choose clubs longer than the standard length because they are tall. Usually a tall person also has long arms, so the added length of the shaft is really not necessary.

The standard weight of a driver is usually listed as D2 or D3. Varying too much from these standard weights can give you tempo problems as you try to control a clubhead that feels like it is leading you, or one so light you are unsure of its location. I have swung clubs that have extreme weight characteristics and find them to be very disconcerting. Stick within the normal weights on your road to improvement.

Drivers vary in clubhead size, and again your choice is mostly a matter of preference. I like a big head on a driver, but I have seen many outstanding players who prefer the compact type. A loft of about eleven degrees is normal for a driver. The key to selecting a driver is feel. When you pick up a club, give the clubhead a little waggle. If it feels right in your hands, then you have probably found the right stick for you. Always try to hit a few balls with your choice before you buy it to see how it feels during the swing and at impact.

Hitting the Driver. Most high handicappers stack the deck against themselves when they are on the tee with a driver in their hands. The most frequent mistakes are:

- Teeing the ball too low
- Poor ball position
- Overswinging
- Lack of confidence

Time and time again, I see the high handicapper tee the ball just off the ground. Because it puts a premium on making contact at a different point, this approach only invites trouble. Remember, the swing with the driver is a sweep in which you strike the ball on the upswing. It is logical to tee the ball high so that the face of the clubhead catches the ball on a slight upswing. With little loft, the driver's face is designed to be hit in this manner. As a rule of thumb, the ball should be teed so that half of it is above the clubface when you set the club on the ground behind the ball. I set the ball in my palm with the tee between my first two fingers in such a way that it enables me to tee at the same height each time.

I spoke about ball positioning earlier, but proper position is never so important as with the driver. For years, I made the mistake of playing the ball too far back in my stance. This position resulted in shots that flew off to the right or simply never got airborne. Move the ball forward so that it is at least even with your left instep. Depending on your swing plane, you may experiment by moving it a shade up or back in order to get the best results. Try to find your ideal position by hitting a lot of shots from the various points near this area. The practice tee is the only place to accomplish this adjustment because one good or bad drive on the course is simply not enough input to make a permanent and important change in your ball position.

When we get a driver in our hands, many of us think of one thing—distance. Particularly among men, distance is an ego thing. Most golfers erroneously equate swinging hard with hitting the long ball. How many times have you hit your worst drive of the day when you really tried to unload? You swing the club back briskly, reach back as far as you can go, then really sing into it during the downswing. The usual result is that the tempo and rhythm are thrown off and the clubhead drifts off the proper swing plane.

To really hit a long ball, you do the opposite. To crank it up, I purposely slow down my back swing and make an extra effort to think "low and slow" during the takeaway. During the downswing, I make an extra effort to delay my wrist release until the very last moment and concentrate on making a full, smooth turn with my shoulders (left shoulder under, right shoulder under). Outside of these slight adjustments, I make no effort to swing harder or move the clubhead faster.

When you stop and think about it, distance is often overrated. In the worst-case scenario, an average drive of 220-240 yards will put you in a position to hit 90 percent of all par fours with a long-iron second shot. On par fives, you still have two more shots to get home to make par. The only times that distance is a significant factor is when you can hit beyond trouble—that is, drive over traps, water, rough, etc.—or set yourself up to hit a short par five in two. If you weighed the two drive characteristics of accuracy and distance, I would opt for accuracy every time. I often watch the tour players hit their drives. I am not overly impressed by their distance, but I marvel at their accuracy off the tee. These players make their living by scoring well. They have the ability to do many things with the driver, but what they choose is to get the ball on the fairway and in a position to get close to the pin on their second shot. I think the message on tee shot and distance is clear: The name of the game is scoring.

The confidence factor seriously affects the ability of the average player to make a good tee shot. There is no magic formula for confidence, but setting up everything for a successful shot beforehand has helped me feel confident with the driver. I set my target line and take a tension-free stance and grip. At this point, I simply think about the word "trust." I trust my swing and trust my club to do the job. Being nervous or worrying about sending the ball into the water or the trees is only programming for failure. Relax and trust yourself. Keep focused on making a smooth, full turn and completing your backswing. Hit your spots and trust your swing.

The Fairway Woods. With a fourteen-club limit, most players opt to carry two fairway woods, usually the 3- and 5-woods. These two clubs, when used correctly, go a long way toward bringing overall improvement to your game. The fairway woods are relatively easy to hit and have many uses. Because of the loft of the clubhead, they are much easier to hit than the driver and long irons, yet they still offer the means to get needed distance.

Fairway wood shots should be played off your left instep, with a stance and swing plane resembling those used with your driver. These clubs are well lofted, with the mass required for distance, so they are ideal for the high handicapper.

The fairway woods require a sweeping motion through impact. Again, concentrate on taking the club back low and smoothly, and deliver the downswing back along the same plane. The woods do require a reasonably good lie. Too often, I see high handicappers who live and die by the sword. They use the 3- or 5-wood any time they are more than 190 yards from the hole, regardless of lie or tightness of the hole.

Faced with a wood shot, I always examine the grass directly behind the ball. Heavy grass directly behind the ball slows down the speed of the club-head and comes between the ball and the clubface. The result is a shot that never gets airborne. I don't know how many times I've seen a guy hit a shot that dribbles a few yards, then walk up to the ball in the rough and try it all over again.

I learned very quickly that when the ball is sitting down it is more productive to hit a 4- or 5-iron out of the rough than a wood. It's just a matter of good sense.

Another common form of fairway wood misuse among high handicappers is what I call *forcing it in.* If you are faced with a 210-yard shot into a green surrounded with trouble, and you try to smack a wood into the green, then you are forcing it in. It's like a quarterback in football trying to hit a receiver who is surrounded by defensive backs. Too many things can go wrong in both situations. As a poor player, this was one of my favorite ways of running up my score. I would often blast away, get into deep trouble, and routinely end up with a double or triple bogey. Remember, because the fairway woods are distance clubs, slight errors on alignment or at impact can throw you off-line quite dramatically. Take a careful look at the target area and evaluate the consequences if you just miss the green—right, left or over. If you can miss the green and make a pitch back from most of the area around the green, then go ahead with the wood. If, on the other hand, there is trouble waiting for you outside the green, then hit a well-placed iron and go for a pitch and one putt. Think of it as saving two or three shots rather than a chickening out of hitting a big one.

When you hit a wood into the green, bounce and roll come into play a great deal. Only greens that are very soft or wet will be able to hold a wood shot. Often, you must plan to land the ball just short and let it run onto the green. You must have the type of approach area in front of the green that will allow you to hit this kind of shot.

On the positive side, the fairway woods offer a great alternative to the driver on many tight holes. Just because the hole is a par four does not mean that you are required to hit the driver. A 3-wood will carry only 20-30 yards shorter than your average drive. On a 380-yard hole, a 230-yard drive with a 1-wood would leave you with a 150-yard 7-iron shot. Using a 3-wood off the tee for accuracy, you up the odds of being on the fairway with a chance of a good iron shot.

Many tight holes have landing areas that are designed to catch drivers in traps, water or rough. Using the 3-wood off the tee avoids the trouble without giving up too much distance. The key to fairway woods is knowing when to use them. My rule of thumb is to always take into consideration the consequences of missing the target. The old cliché, "It's not *how*, but *how many*," should come to mind whenever you are contemplating using the fairway woods. They are great tools when used at the right time, but they can bring you a lot of trouble if you don't evaluate everything involved in making the wood shot.

The Irons

Hitting long, straight iron shots was always a mystery to me. For every good shot I hit, there would be three others that would not fly right, skim low along the ground, or worse, dribble a few yards after I had slammed the clubhead into the ground behind the ball. I knew that if I was to become a good golfer, it would be essential that, when I stepped up over an iron shot, I would know what I was doing and where the shot was going.

Watching the poor golfers' swings instead of the pros' gave me insight into my own problems. I continually noticed that high handicappers seemed to have two different swings. Using the driver or fairway woods, they seemed to make a long arc and a reasonable attempt at the shoulder-turn. With the iron shots, however, these same players become arm-and hand-swingers. Even during the setup, I noticed their hands were often behind the ball at address where they have been in front on the tee shot. When I stopped to think about these observations, I came to some conclusions.

First of all, when we step up to an iron shot, we are placing a premium on accuracy. We are looking at a pinpoint target rather than an area target. In a poor golfer, the need for accuracy is somehow translated into controlling the club with the arms and hands. Secondly, we all want iron shots that rise up high and settle down gently on the green. Among high handicappers, the need to get the ball into the air quickly also leads to the misuse of hands. Finally, because irons have shorter shafts, the poor golfer subconsciously perceives the need for a full turn and backswing as unnecessary.

The use of hands and arms in iron shots is manifested in several ways. In order to guide the clubhead to the ball, the high handicapper virtually eliminates foot movement, hip-turn and shoulder-turn. To get the ball up quickly, many golfers employ some kind of scooping action in their swing with the irons. They seem to be trying to help the ball get into the air by breaking their wrists early in an attempt to loft the ball from the turf. These movements are actually 180 degrees from what you need to hit those clean, crisp iron shots that fly high and true.

The first thing I needed to do was to take an inventory of my swing with the irons. Using the full-length mirror, I took my usual setup and made an honest swing—swinging as I would normally swing during actual play. As I made swing after swing, two things became evident. I was playing the ball way up in the front of my stance, and I was hardly turning my shoulders or hips. Compared to my swing with the driver, I was flat-footed. In examining videotapes of the swings of touring pros, it became obvious that their swings with the irons were essentially the same as with their woods. In particular, I noted that the position of their hands and the amount of shoulder-turn were the same. The only differences came in the areas of stance, ball position, downswing arc and the strike of the ball.

In molding my swing, I again concentrated on my spots. I worked on getting my hands up high at the top and making the "left shoulder under, right shoulder under" move.

For the mid irons (4, 5, 6), I play the ball in the middle of my stance. Long irons (2, 3) are played off of my left heel, while I hit the short irons slightly right of center. This ball position allows for the changes dictated by shaft-length. For the long irons, the swing is essentially the same as the fairway woods, producing a long, low arc in the backswing and a sweeping stroke for the downswing.

The middle and short irons require a different approach because of what happens at impact. While watching the touring pros hit their iron shots in practice, I carefully studied the ball as the clubhead struck it. The impact created by the touring pros was completely different from what I experienced or what I had observed in most amateur players. In hitting the mid and short irons, the touring pros would strike the ball with more of a pinching action than a hitting action. They would strike with a descending blow, the clubhead reaching its lowest point several inches in front of the ball. The clubhead would pinch the ball, then drive on through, taking a divot in front of where the ball had been. There was no sweeping, scooping or slapping.

The swing used for the mid and short irons is made with the same backswing characteristics as mentioned earlier. Because of the shorter shaft, however, the clubhead and shaft will not extend to the parallel position at the top. To achieve my spot position, I simply concentrated on making my shoulder-turn once, getting my hands up high. Once my left shoulder was under my chin and my left arm was fully extended back, I had completed my backswing and was set to start my downswing.

The downswing for the mid and short irons is a relatively sharp descending blow. I learned to hold my wrist release until the last possible moment by concentrating on pulling down with my hands from the top of the swing. The clubface should strike the ball downward, as if you are trying to pinch the ball out of the ground. I concentrate on driving the clubface down and through the ball, taking a good divot in front of the ball, and keeping the clubface driving along the target line. I intentionally guard against quitting on the ball or just getting the clubhead through and leaving it there. I make sure I continue through the ball with a full turn and follow-through.

By adjusting stance and ball position, you are allowing for the differences in shaft-length. For the mid irons, I stand with my feet slightly inside my shoulders, my left foot turned slightly toward the target and my right foot perpendicular to the target line. For the short irons, my stance becomes slightly more narrow, but slightly more open. I learned to open the stance (left foot slightly away from the target line) in order to facilitate a full turn. Because the shaft is shorter on the 7-, 8- and 9-irons, you need a quick turning action. The open stance eliminates any quick, jerky turns and allows you to pivot evenly and smoothly onto your left side.

One of the key reasons why high handicappers have trouble hitting good iron shots is that they do not get their weight shifted properly. I realized this early in my makeover program and have made the following adjustments with my irons:

- As I set up over the ball, I have slightly more weight on my left side to emphasize the feeling that I want to achieve at impact.

- I set up so that my left shoulder and clubface form a straight diagonal line to the ball, enabling me to establish a feeling of a strong left side and emphasizing a solid one-piece takeaway driven by left-side movement.

- At the top of the swing, I make a sliding movement with my hips to facilitate the transfer of my weight to the left side.

- I make sure that my right shoulder comes under my chin before my head comes up.

- Just before impact, I create the feeling that my right hand is snapping through and driving the clubface after my wrist release.

- I make sure that my right shoulder comes under my chin before my head comes up.

Another small but important difference I observed between high handicappers and touring pros is how they position the clubface at address. Most missed shots off the clubs of high handicappers appear to land to the right of the target. Many average golfers address the ball with the clubface open. The touring pro, on the other hand, has his clubface square or even slightly closed. By checking myself in the mirror, I was able to see that I also had an open clubface at address.

Most of us think that we have a square clubface setup, but the perception is an optical illusion. This false perception occurs because of the way an iron rises from the hosel, or heel, to the toe of the club. I check this fault by imagining a fine line running down the target line and through the ball. I then imagine a crossline running perpendicular to the target line and crossing the ball. I line my clubface along that line. In practice, you can actually use tape or string to check graphically if you are indeed setting up with an open clubface.

Choosing Your Irons. Recent design changes in irons have created clubs that are much easier to hit with. Clubs with a wide flange (bottom), such as the Ping and Dunlop models, help prevent the clubface from bouncing or turning as it strikes the ground. The wide flange helps the club flow at impact and gets the ball into the air more easily. Many of these clubs also have heel-toe weighting characteristics that help eliminate the twisting of shots hit slightly off-center. In other words, they create a larger sweet spot. For the high handicapper setting out on a program of improvement, these clubs offer a real advantage.

The long irons, because of their long shafts and low loft, are particularly difficult clubs to use. They require a sweeping stroke, much like the fairway woods. For the high handicapper, I would recommend using the 4-and 5-woods as replacements for the 2- and 3-irons until you have developed a solid, full swing. I did not touch my 2- and 3-irons until I had developed my new swing. Through practice and the development of an upright swing plane, I now prefer my long irons over the woods. In fact, I now carry a 1-iron and often use it when the situation calls for a long accurate shot. As for woods, I carry only a driver and a 3-wood in my bag. The message is to hold back on the long irons while you develop. Eventually, with practice and improvement, the long irons will become a welcome addition to your repertoire.

Lastly, a good iron shot should be preceded by an evaluation of the texture of the turf. With medium and short irons you drive through the turf, so variations in texture can greatly affect the shot. If the ground is wet and soft, you must guard against driving the clubhead too deeply after the strike of the ball. In this situation, try to set your swing plane so that after you strike the ball, your club drives down and under the top roots of the grass. Take a divot, but make sure your club drives on through and not down. Sometimes you may find your ball on a spongy turf caused by intertwined roots. In this case, it is difficult to cut through the roots, so a sweeping action at impact rather than a down-and-through motion is best. On hardpan, or hard, dry ground, the clubhead will tend to bounce rather than drive through. Take a club with a little more loft, stay down and expect the club to bounce as you hit down and through the ball. You should grip a little more firmly in this situation to prevent the club from twisting or turning at impact.

6

THE SCORING SHOTS

The scoring shots, to me, are those golf shots that separate the good golfer from the hacker. They are those shots that enable you to save par, salvage a bogey and, on occasion, make a birdie. Many instruction books refer to putting and chipping as the scoring shots, but for the high handicapper most of the scoring doesn't take place on the green but on the way to it. For the pro, putting makes up about half his score; for the high handicapper, putting constitutes about a third of his shots.

If you cannot execute the scoring shots, you will be looking at a double bogey or worse. When faced with a difficult situation, the poor player too often concedes the hole. The good player, on the other hand, not only knows how to make these shots but practices them on a regular basis. It is imperative that you learn how to make these shots. I made a list of all the difficult, critical and pressure shots that seriously affect scoring. I set out to learn how to execute these shots, then practiced them until they became part of my game.

The Wedges

In order to focus on the shots that have a major impact on our scores, I have categorized them as: wedges, sand shots, fairway shots and other scoring shots. From 120 yards on into the green, the use or misuse of the wedge is critical to scoring. As a poor golfer, I would hit a wide assortment of bad shots with the wedge. I was never quite sure if I was going to skull one over the green or hit a high floater that bounced all over the green to leave me with a 40-foot putt. Since the high handicapper misses a lot of greens, the wedge is a frequently used club.

Being able to place wedge shots near the pin consistently can save strokes in bunches. The type of wedge shot you should hit is determined by your target area. For example, if the greens are holding (soft greens that allow the ball to stop quickly), I go with a pitching wedge, sending the ball high and directly toward the target. Establish the target line based on where you want the ball to land. I always try to read the green, selecting the position that will leave me with the easiest putt. Going right at the pin is not always the best policy. I select a landing zone for the ball and then visualize how the shot will react based on the slope and speed of the green.

The Full Wedge Shot. To set up for the full wedge shot, I use a narrow, open stance, which creates an upright swing with a sharply descending downstroke. A good wedge shot should sit down quickly and not bounce all over the green. It is much easier to fly the ball to a point on the green and make it stop than it is to rely on a ball that bounces and rolls. To hit the kind of wedge that flies to an area and stops, you must hit it with backspin. Creating backspin is not as difficult as it may appear. To create spin, I take a normal back-swing, pull down sharply on the downswing and snap my right hand through at impact. The secret to good backspin is to catch the ball cleanly with a downward motion of the clubhead that pinches the ball from the turf. The club should take a divot in front of the ball then stay directly along the target line. Practice this shot by pinching shots at a very short distance of, say, 50 yards, then gradually move the shots farther out after you have developed the snap and pinch that produces spin. Concentrate on hitting the ball cleanly, with a solid movement of the clubface that goes down and through the ball. Avoid the tendency to scoop the ball into the air, which is counterproductive to creating backspin.

The Cut Wedge. One shot that has really helped me to score well is the cut wedge shot, which I use when I need to lift the ball over trouble and land it softly on the green without much bounce or roll. I set up with a narrow, open stance and an opened clubface. The sand wedge is perfect for this shot as you do not need to drive down and through the ball. Because the sand wedge's flange is wide and beveled, it skims under the ball instead of digging into the turf. I take the club back slightly outside of the target line and return it to the ball in an outside-in manner (*see figure 15*). Let the club do the work; the ball will pop up high and float down to the green. This shot is best used when you are within 50 yards of the pin. You will need a good lie in order to lift the ball, so do not attempt to cut a ball from a lead lie in which the ball is embedded deeply.

The Punch Shot. The punch shot is a nice little shot to have in your bag of tricks. Setup is similar to the full-wedge setup. The key to hitting the punch shot is the wrists. Take a normal backswing with one less club than normal. On your downswing, hold your hands so that you do not snap them through impact. Instead, let the wrists break slightly, with the left hand lead-ing through the shot instead of having the right hand hitting the ball. As you strike the ball, keep the clubhead low to the ground through the follow-through and hold it along the target line. Strive for a feeling of having your hands in a firm position throughout the swing.

The punch shot is an ideal shot for going into the wind or hitting a low shot from under a tree. I have noticed that many pros now use the punch shot as an approach shot because of its accuracy. As you practice this shot, concentrate on keeping the clubface along the target line back and through impact. Always check to make sure that the clubface is square and that your grip is slightly more firm than usual.

After learning this shot and practicing with it for about a week, I went out to play a round. On the very first hole, my drive ended up behind a tree, about 150 yards from the green. I hit a low, punched shot that zoomed

figure 15

A Hacker No More

under the branches of the tree, rose up and landed about four feet from the pin. It was a great feeling of satisfaction to learn a shot, master it and then use it in play to save strokes. Only a few weeks earlier, I would have hit a grounder under the tree, then pitched onto the green.

Judging Distance with the Wedge. One of the things that perplexed me most about the wedge shot was determining how hard to hit the ball. It seemed that I was always either flying the ball over the green or leaving it very short. After a while, I had become so paranoid about hitting wedge shots that I often had trouble pulling the trigger. Many times I ended up "chilly-dipping" or slamming the club into the ground behind the ball because of tension. I decided to investigate how good golfers judge distance and hit the shot with the proper amount of force.

The touring pros seem to spend more time over wedge shots than over a 5-iron from 175 yards out. They take several more practice swings than with other clubs. The top players find the yardage to the target by using prede-termined markers (bush, rock) that they pace off beforehand. Sometimes they have their caddies pace off the distance if time permits. Once they establish how much yardage there is to the target, they know how hard to hit the ball. Yet knowing how hard to hit the ball is not merely a matter of feel. Several good golfers told me that they "calibrate" their swings with the wedge to produce the proper amount of distance. In practice, you may cal-ibrate distance by taking the club back to different points in your back-swing. For example, swing the club halfway into your backswing and hit through the ball with your normal downswing. Note the distance the ball carries as you repeat this shot over and over. This "setting" should produce a standard amount of carry that you can use as a base. To add distance, increase the amount of backswing; to reduce distance, make a shorter back-swing. From practice, you will be able to determine the spots in your back-swing that translate into specific amounts of carry. When you see the tour-ing pros taking practice swings with the wedge, they are actually rehearsing the distance that they will take the club back based on how far they want the ball to travel.

Sand Shots

Sand traps present a double threat to the high handicapper. First, he dreads getting into the sand because he has so much trouble getting out; sec-ond, his approach shots suffer from the tension created by the presence of a sand trap along the target line. The shot from the sand is not a particularly dif-ficult one; compared to most other "trouble" shots, it is actually relatively easy. The sand shot is mostly a matter of mechanics. If you think correctly and make the correct movements, the ball will come up and out every time.

The Swing for the Sand Shot. The swing plane for the sand shot should be very upright. As you take the club back, release your wrists early in order to create a sharp arc. The distance that the ball will travel is determined by the length of the backswing, but it should be full enough so that you do not make a jerky, fast swing into the ball. On the downswing, let your hands lead through and stay ahead of the clubface. Keep the head still and follow through.

To hit the sand shot properly, swing in a slow, deliberate manner and let the club do the work. The slow, deliberate swing prevents your hands from burying the club in the sand or skulling the ball over the green. To promote a deliberate swing, I usually slow down all my movements as I walk up to a sand shot. As I step up to the ball, I hold the swing thought, "nice and slow." The worst thing that you can do in the trap is to try to scoop the ball out with your hands. The sand shot is the only shot in golf in which you do not focus on the ball. I look at the spot where the club will strike the sand. For a normal sand shot, you should have the club strike about two inches behind the ball. Let the club pass under the ball and come out on the other side, along the target line. The clubface does not come in contact with the ball; it causes the sand to propel the ball up and out of the trap. I like to think of cutting a slice of sand out from under the ball, or *spooning* the ball out (*see figure 16*).

figure 16

A Hacker No More

The reason that you should let the club do the work is that the sand wedge is especially designed for its job of cutting through sand. The lead edge of the sand wedge is made to cut into the sand evenly and smoothly. The flange of the sand wedge is beveled so that the club will skim through the sand without becoming embedded. A sand wedge with a moderate flange is best as it offers more versatility, such as shots from different textures of sand or from the fairway. Sand wedges that have very large flanges are usually only good for traps with very coarse sand.

Setup. For the basic sand shot, play the ball off your left heel and stand fairly close to the ball to promote an upright swing plane. Open the face of the sand wedge so that, almost flat, it approaches the horizontal plane of the trap itself. Open your stance by pulling your left foot back from the target line and open your hips and shoulders slightly to the left as well. The shot does not require much of a shoulder-turn as it is made mostly with the arms and hands.

As you take your stance in the trap, dig your feet well into the sand. This movement serves two purposes: it anchors you into the sand so that you will not slip or sway as you swing, and it allows you to test the sand for consistency. On occasion, you may find a trap that has light, fluffy sand on top but heavy, wet sand just an inch or two underneath. It is the bottom sand that affects your club the most, so it is smart to gather as much information on the sand as possible.

You should grip the sand wedge a little more firmly than usual. You need a firm grip to prevent the club from turning in your hands as it goes through the sand. I like to grip the sand wedge with the fingers of my left hand, promoting a desirable wristy swing.

Wet Sand. Often, traps do not drain well and the sand remains wet and heavy. The ball tends to go farther out of wet sand because the clubhead does not dig as deeply as it would in soft, dry sand. The clubhead skims closer to the ball as it passes under. The swing should be made with a firm grip, a slightly opened face and a slow, smooth swing with a strong follow-through. Time and time again, I have seen the high handicapper try to pick the ball clean from wet sand. This shot is extremely difficult and more often than not results in disaster.

Downhill Lie in the Sand. If the ball is on a downslope in the trap, you will need to compensate for the lie. As you set up, dig deeply into the sand to get a solid base. Put your weight on your back foot to prevent swaying. You will need to enter the sand with the clubhead a little farther from the ball than normal to allow for the slope. Open the clubface to a wide position and keep the club moving under the ball. There is a strong tendency to scoop the ball in this situation, so remain disciplined and make the proper swing to loft the ball out.

Fried Egg. If the ball is in the middle of a little crater caused by the sand flying away as the ball lands, then you have what is called a *fried egg*. These lies usually only occur in soft sand, but they can be tricky. The danger of this lie is that the clubface may bounce off the rim of the crater and into the ball. To guard against this, hold your focus on the spot where your club will enter the sand. Come into that spot with a sharp descending stroke, then keep the club moving along the target line. Make sure you follow through by having the club finish well up from the sand. Remember to keep a steady head and a firm grip and to make a full deliberate swing, letting the club do the work.

Embedded Ball. If the ball is embedded in the sand with just the top of it visible, you will need a sharp, descending blow to cut under the ball. The stroke is sharper, more like a "knife" than a "spoon" (*see figure 17*). The stroke requires more power, but do not try to muscle the ball out. Remain smooth and swing with enough power to have the club glide completely under the ball. If the sand is coarse or heavy, it might be advisable to use a pitching wedge or 9-iron and to move the ball back toward the center of your stance. Close the face of the club slightly to help you dig into the sand better.

Soft Explosion. If the ball is in a trap very close to the pin, you need to get it up and out and then have the ball settle down quickly. This is certainly a finesse shot. I like to open the face of the wedge as much as possible and

figure 17

A Hacker No More

make a rather wide arc in which I skim just a little sand from under the ball and finish with a short follow-through. The swing is slow and smooth, and I have the feeling of serving up the ball rather than blasting it from the sand. Because it involves touch, this shot requires a lot of practice. On the PGA Tour, players often spend a lot of time on this shot every day to develop a feel for it.

Fairway Bunkers. A fairway bunker shot requires the same swing as a normal fairway shot with a few modifications. In making a full swing from the sand, I dig my feet in well to prevent sliding. When feet are locked into the sand, foot action is severely restricted, so the swing becomes more of an arm and shoulder swing. I try to concentrate on making a full turn and pulling down with my left side. The key to hitting a good fairway trap shot is to strike the ball first, and then take a "divot" of sand from in front of the ball. Most problems with this shot occur as a result of hitting behind the ball. Focus on the ball and concentrate on striking it cleanly on the downstroke. A good idea is to take one more club than necessary as the sand tends to slow clubhead speed at impact.

Any iron may be hit from a fairway trap, but special care must be taken when using a wood. In order to hit a wood from a trap, you need a low clearance. The ball will fly out at a low trajectory, so any kind of lip of the trap must be taken into consideration. A particular problem occurs if the wood strikes the sand behind the ball; it bounces into the ball. As a general rule, I go with a long iron in this situation unless conditions are absolutely perfect for a wood shot.

Sand traps are a part of the game, and knowing how to play out of the sand is an essential part of becoming a complete golfer. To ignore this part of the game is to concede to an easy opponent. Touring pros get out of a trap and one-putt a green more than 50 percent of the time. The number of shots you can save, not to mention the improvement to your mental framework, is truly significant. Just think of how your scores would improve if you could get out of a sand trap every time with only one or two putts needed to finish the hole. As sand shots are mostly a matter of mechanics, this goal is well within your reach.

Out of the Rough

Too often, I feel, we forget our objective once we find ourselves in heavy rough. Our efforts from the rough should focus on one thing—getting out. This area can send your scores soaring, so you must take care. As a poor scorer, I would set up over a shot from heavy rough with the intention of hitting the green. Usually, my swing thought was to swing hard, to power the clubface through the heavy grass. More often than not, the result was a shot that skimmed along the ground and remained in the rough. This common fault of the high handicapper is a combination of bad technique and poor thinking. By trying to power the ball from the rough, you have a natural tendency to cast your hands from the top instead of pulling down into the shot. In studying how good players approach the shot from the rough, I learned that my approach was way off base. There are different strategies depending on the type of rough that you are faced with in your shot.

Heavy Rough. Heavy rough is thick, coarse grass in which your ball settles down into a deep lie. In this situation, your primary goal should be to get the ball onto the fairway and in position to hit the green with your next shot. I remember watching a PGA Tour event at La Costa in Carlsbad, California, at which the pros were using sand wedges to pitch back to the fairway because of the dense rough. The message: think of scoring first and foremost.

In a shot from heavy rough, the grass tends to grab at the clubface as it comes into the ball, causing it to slow down and twist. Grass thrusts between the clubface and the ball, deadening the shot at impact, costing distance and negating backspin. High grass also grabs at the ball as it starts out on its flight, creating the danger of leaving the ball in the same predicament in which you started.

The pros at La Costa knew that the only option was simply to get out of the rough to the nearest point of the fairway. In a similar situation, you should approach the shot as if you were making an explosion shot from the sand. Using a sand wedge, open your stance and bring the club down sharply, right at the ball. The sharp downward blow lessens the amount of grass impeding your club on the way to the ball. At impact, try to catch the ball under the bottom so that it pops up high and eliminates the chance of the grass catching the ball on its ascent. You need to grip the club firmly to prevent twisting and to provide the force to cut through the grass. It is important to follow through completely so that you do not leave the clubface at the ball. A sharp descending blow with a good follow-through will get the job done nicely.

One point that I always keep in mind while playing out of rough is never to sole the club. Often, the ball is balanced on blades of grass, and there is a good chance that placing the club behind the ball will cause it to move. This, of course, results in a penalty stroke. By holding the clubhead a few inches above the ground, it also becomes easier to make a more upright backswing, eliminating the possibility of catching grass with your club during thetakeaway.

Medium Rough. Most courses today have what can be described as medium rough. The long, thick rough found at major championships would seriously slow down play and serve as too severe a penalty for the average golfer who strays from the fairway. Most courses have a two-to-three-inch rough that produces lies where the ball sits low into the grass or, in some cases, on top of thickly matted grass. Both situations require specific strategies.

One of my favorite shots from a tight lie in the rough is the punch. I set up with the ball slightly back in my stance. With a slightly opened clubface, I make a high arc in the backswing and hit down hard with a chopping blow. The ball usually comes out on a line drive with a good roll. This is a great shot for the times when you cannot reach the green by getting the ball up high. Instead, plan on having the ball run onto the green much as you would in a pitch-and-run shot.

For a lie in the rough in which I can see a great deal of the ball, I modify my normal setup. I select a club with more loft than would be required from a normal lie. The added loft is in response to two considerations. First, I need to get the ball up quickly to avoid the grass in front of the ball, and second, because it has little backspin, a ball coming out of the rough will run a great deal. I open the clubface slightly as the rough tends to close the clubface as the grass grabs near the hosel. With a firm grip and a sharp, descending blow, I concentrate on staying down on the shot and making a smooth follow-through. Because of the open clubface and extra loft, the ball will tend to fly high and fade. I usually try to land the ball in front of the green and let the ball run on; it is very difficult to have a ball hold a green from the rough.

If the ball is sitting up on top of thick, coarse grass, special care is required. This is the kind of lie that will produce a *flyer.* A flyer is a ball that travels like a knuckleball through the air and often sails well over the target. In this situation, I take at least one less club than is required and concentrate on hitting the ball first, then having the club skim through the grass in front of the ball. The danger with this type of lie is hitting under the ball and causing a high pop-up, or hitting the ball solidly on the upswing, creating a flyer.

Most rough shots should not be a major problem if you remember the proper technique. The biggest problem that I have observed among high handicappers is the tendency to try to power the ball out with the hands alone. Stay smooth by pulling down with the left side and use a downstroke that descends sharply to the ball, lifting the ball up and out quickly. When faced with a shot from the rough, your first concern should be scoring. In other words, decide what you need to do in order to avoid trouble and put yourself in a position to make par or, at worst, bogey. Trying to make a career shot out of the rough puts too much pressure on you and creates unneeded tension in the swing. Getting out of the rough is more a matter of brains than brawn.

On the Slopes

While sand and rough can create difficult shot situations, the fairway also presents us with some real challenges. Of all the fairway shots, the sloping lie seems to instill a particular dread in the high handicapper. While playing in a match several years ago, I had a 9-iron shot from a steep downhill lie to a fast green. I remember running through all the things that I had read about such lies as I stood over the ball. I could feel the tension rise in my hands and arms as my brain worked overtime telling me what I should be doing. My partner must have thought that I had slipped into some kind of transcendental trance as I stood frozen in the address position. I had become frozen from the pressure that I had put on myself. I finally jerked the club back and hit a screamer over the right-hand side of the green. I remember this shot distinctly because it taught me a good lesson about difficult shots. I had a good idea of what I should do in that situation, but I did not know how the swing, weight transfer and impact would feel. The answer was to practice downhill lies until they became second nature to me.

Simply saying "practice them" may seem trite, but in the case of these special shots, a great deal of attention is required. Now, be honest—have you ever gone to a practice area or driving range and hit nothing but downhill lie shots? Before freezing over that 9-iron shot, my answer was obviously no. I could not remember ever practicing a downhill shot with intensity at any time in my life. It may be a lot more fun to smack the driver than to hit downhill lies, but I realized that I had to look at the big picture. Do I have fun now at practice, or do I learn how to hit a downhill lie shot so that my overall game is strengthened? Practice enabled me to link confidence and feel to technique in order to play these shots well. I had to scout around my area to find a practice place that had a slope, but the search was worthwhile.

In hitting shots that put you at an angle, the main consideration is gravity. We are comfortable hitting a ball on a level lie because the laws of gravity do not disturb our normal swings in any particular way. On the other hand, a sloping lie affects our swings in several ways. We affect our weight shift by either accelerating or restricting our movement from one foot to the other, or from our heels to our toes. The angle that the club-head travels toward the ball is changed by the slope of the hill and the effects of gravity.

To hit a good shot from a sloping lie, we must reverse the effects of gravity. In other words, the adjustments that we make should create a normal sense of balance and swing plane by acting against what gravity is trying to do to us.

Downhill Lie. When the slope of the hill forces your weight onto your left foot, you must be careful not to sway off the ball, topping the shot or striking the ground behind the ball (fat shot). To adjust to the slope and gravity, I try to reverse their effects. I set up with the ball back a few more inches than normal to allow for the change in the swing plane. Because of the slope of the hill, the low part of your swing will occur at a point a few inches to the right of your normal spot with a level lie. To negate the effects of gravity, I set my weight on my back foot and make sure to hold it there throughout the swing. I set my hips and shoulders in a position that is level. Setting your weight back on your right foot is not enough by itself to overcome the effects of the slope. By setting your hips and shoulders on a level plane, you take away the hill's effect and normalize your stance approach. The moment of truth in a downhill shot is the drive down through impact. By staying back on my right side, I have the feeling of driving down and through the ball with my hands and arms instead of the usual full shoulder-turn and sliding movement in the hips. The key is to concentrate on keeping a steady head through impact. If your head remains still, you will not swing off the ball. Stay down to the shot and let the clubhead fire out toward the target after impact.

On a downhill lie, trust the club to get the ball into the air. Trying to scoop the ball will only result in a topped shot. Since the swing plane is heading downward, the flight of the ball will be lower and the ball will run farther. By taking a club with more loft, you will give yourself an easier shot and allow for the added distance from the low trajectory and increased roll. The slope of the hill will also cause your ball to fade from left to right. Allow for this by setting up your target line to the left of your intended landing area. For short approach shots, you should keep in mind that there will be little backspin, and the ball will bounce and roll farther than normal.

Uphill Lie. The uphill shot is generally easier to hit than the downhill, but there are still some problem areas that require adjustment. The major problem on the uphill shot occurs during the backswing, when the weight is shifted to the right side. Often, the player experiences a loss of balance. Many times the high handicapper does not get his weight back onto the left side and ends up topping the ball or hitting a vicious pull-hook.

Adjust to the uphill shot by using principles opposite to the downhill technique. Play the ball up in your stance to adjust to the slope of the hill. I close my stance and aim to the right of the target as the ball will draw from right to left. I place my weight on the left side by standing so that I feel like I am pushing into the hill with my left foot. I brace myself with the inside of my right foot. I guard against getting my weight on the outside of my right foot. I set my shoulders and hips on the level to give myself a feeling of making as normal a swing as possible. The swing plane should follow the slope of the hill. It is important to sweep the ball from the uphill lie, taking only a small divot, so that the club will not dig into the side of the hill. Don't fight the hill—go with it. Take one more club than necessary as the ball will fly high and settle down quickly.

In hitting a wedge from an uphill lie, I would sometimes end up with a high pop-up shot that would land well short of my target. The punch shot also works for the uphill approach. I simply take a less lofted club and, with an upright backswing, hit straight down and through the ball with a descending blow. This shot requires less effort, is usually very accurate and does not involve the shifting of weight that can lead to trouble. You should practice this one special shot—it has been a big help to me.

Side Hill Lie—Ball Below the Feet. This particular shot can be one of the most difficult shots in golf. With this lie you must resist the forces that pull you toward the ball during the swing. You should set your target line to the left of your intended landing area as the ball will move from left to right. In aiming to the left, make sure that your alignment is square and that your stance is not open. I grip the club at the very end and stand closer to the ball than normal.

One thing that has helped me with this shot is keeping my legs *soft*. By this, I mean flexing my knees and keeping my legs flexible to help me stay balanced and down to the ball during the swing. As I set up, I try to feel that my weight is set back on my heels and I concentrate on maintaining a center of balance in the middle of my body.

Side Hill Lie—Ball Above the Feet. Just by the nature of this shot, your swing must become very flat. To compensate for this, the best strategy is to use an open stance, choke up on the club and stand upright. The ball will tend to hook from this lie, so you should aim to the right of your target. I also maintain a firm left hand to prevent it from rolling over at impact and causing a sheet-faced hook. The ball should be struck cleanly as there is a tendency to dig the club into the side of the hill.

The shots from the various hilly situations described above require some adjustment to the pre-shot routine. I normally do not take a full practice swing before I play a shot, but with sloping lies I find that it is essential. By taking a practice swing, you get a sense of how the force of gravity will impact as you swing. You can also note where your club strikes the ground. This will help you set your ball position based on the swing plane that is created by the slope.

Other Scoring Shots

The High Shot. The high shot has become one of my favorite shots for getting out of trouble or cutting distance on a dogleg. I naturally hit the ball high, but with a few adjustments I am able to get the ball up very quickly to clear trouble. To hit this shot, play the ball well up in your stance and open both your stance and the clubface. I try to stay behind the ball and release my wrists so that the right hand snaps into the ball at impact, strikes the ball first, and then takes turf in front of the ball. The ball should pop up quickly and fade slightly, so you should aim to the left of your target.

The Low Shot. Many times during the golf season, you will be faced with having to hit a shot under trees to get out of trouble. This shot is relatively easy to make but also easy to mishit by high handicappers with poor technique. The ball should be played back in the stance with a low-lofted club. Too often, I see golfers try to hit this shot with a wedge or 9-iron. I use a 4-iron and regulate my distance by the length of the backswing. Take a long, low backswing straight along the target line. Make the downswing with the hands held firmly and the clubface kept low and straight along the target line during the follow-through. The key is to avoid a wristy swing that causes the ball to pop into the air.

Ball in Divot. Life's unfair. So you just hit one 250 yards down the middle, only to find your ball in a divot. Stay calm; this situation has happened to everyone who plays the game, and it is not a major problem. I have had the best success in this situation using a punch shot that goes after the ball in the divot and drives it out. Make an upright backswing and come into the ball sharply to pinch the ball up and out. Open your stance slightly and grip the club a little more firmly with the left hand. Take time to practice this shot, as it will come in handy more times than you expect. It may not be fun to practice, but it is a great shot to have in your bag.

Hitting a Fade. The intentional fade is a valuable shot to have in your repertoire. Many touring pros work the ball from left to right on almost all of their approach shots because of the fade's tendency to sit down quickly. It is not a shot that is restricted to experts only; it can be mastered with a few simple adjustments and practice.

Because of bad advice, I struggled with this shot for years. I would change my grip to a "weak" position and try to make an outside-in swing. These changes were just too much for me to handle. On the advice of a teaching pro, I learned a much easier technique that produced consistent results. I line up so that my target line is left of my

figure 18

A Hacker No More

intended landing area (*see figure 18*). All that is required now is to open the face of the club to set the amount of fade required. Make sure you avoid turning your hands to open the clubface at address. Your hands will correct themselves during the swing by rolling back to a square position and sending the ball left of your target. To take the proper grip for the fade, I use the following method:

- Lay the clubhead squarely behind the ball and toward the target left of your landing area.

- With the index finger and thumb of your right hand, turn the clubface to set the amount of fade required.

- Hold the clubface in this position and take a normal grip that leaves the face open.

Once you have your setting and alignment, take your normal swing. There is no need to make an outside-in swing as the open clubface will do the work for you. As you practice this shot, note the flight characteristics produced by the amount of openness that you place in the clubface.

On the course, I use the fade for my 5-iron through 9-iron shots, as it offers a great deal of control and stops quickly on the green. It is also a great shot to use when you are faced with a shot that requires you to come into a pin guarded in front by a trap. As a trouble shot, it will enable you to go around trees and verticals instead of risking shots that go over or under them.

Hitting the Draw. In order to hit a draw or hook, make the opposite manipulations. Set your target line to the right of your intended landing area (*see figure 19*) and keep the clubface closed. Set the club in the same way as you did for the intentional fade by closing the face with the thumb and index finger of your right hand. Take a normal swing and let the club do the work. The spin created by the closed clubface will cause the ball to move from right to left, so there is no need for extracurricular efforts to draw the club inside-out during the swing.

The hooked or drawn ball will tend to run after it lands, so make allowances when you select your landing area and the amount of club. On fairways that are cut low or burned out, the draw from the tee will add considerable distance to your drive. As a trouble shot, the draw offers the same benefits as the fade. I have hooked the ball from the first day I played, so use this shot with a great deal of caution and only when conditions are perfect.

Playing in the Wind. Wind conditions seem to affect poor players more than good golfers. The high handicapper usually makes adjustments for

figure 19

A Hacker No More

wind play that are counterproductive and self-defeating. After I began to play well, I had an unusually poor round while playing in high winds. My poor round was not caused by the wind pushing my shots as much as my attempts to compensate for the wind. I vowed that I would never let the wind intimidate me into playing poorly again. I decided to learn how to play sensibly in the wind.

My first step was to disregard some commonly held notions about wind play. For example, a long-held principle of wind play is to tee the ball high with a following wind and tee low against the wind. While this may work for some, it did not make good golfing sense to me. By teeing the ball high or low, you change your swing plane and ball position to make solid contact. Playing in the wind is difficult enough without adding the increased pressure of adjusting to new tee settings while on the course. If the wind is against you, the key is to make solid contact with the ball. By teeing the ball low, you invite a host of problems. For one thing, a low shot hit with side spin (hook or slice) will be accentuated. In baseball, a pitcher who has a good curve or slice loves to pitch against the wind—his ball will break much more effectively. On the golf course, a low drive with side spin into the wind leads to big trouble. I tee the ball normally and concentrate on making solid contact.

A common indication of wind intimidation is overswinging. Against the wind, there is a natural tendency to feel that we must crunch the ball in order for it to cut through the wind. With a strong wind following, we cannot resist the urge to set distance records by getting our drives high up into the wind. If anything, I have learned that the secret to good wind play is to stay smooth and swing normally in both situations. The wind condition is simply part of the course. It exists for everyone playing on that day, and for every yard it takes away, it will probably give it back. By setting your mind at ease and playing the course as it is, your chances are immediately improved for better play in the wind.

In speaking with several good players about playing in the wind, I gained several good tips. When playing into a strong wind, many good players set up with their weight slightly on their left side instead of being equally balanced. This adjustment shortens the backswing slightly—a measure against overswinging. It also helps to ensure solid contact with the ball.

In crosswinds, good players tend to work the ball into the wind. For example, if you are faced with a "nine o'clock" crosswind, it may be a good idea to fade the ball into the wind rather than have the wind work on a straight shot.

There is no strict table for the amount of club required for various wind speeds, but a good rule of thumb is to drop or add one club for every ten miles per hour of wind. You should try to figure out how the wind is affecting your shot during your pre-round practice. Special care needs to be taken for the short irons (7-iron through wedge), as the ball will tend to hang up in the air longer and thus be affected more by the wind. On very windy days, I have gone to hitting the punch shot in these situations, because the ball will stay low and straight and spend less time in the wind. For close-in shots, the pitch-and-run shot is preferable to the high lob.

7

TROUBLESHOOTING

The best auto mechanics are the good troubleshooters. When you bring your car in and describe a particular noise or problem, he focuses on several likely problem areas in your engine to take remedial action. In golf, when things go wrong with our swing they manifest themselves in such ways as slices, hooks or topped shots. We have to identify the cause of the problem, which we do by troubleshooting. Being a troubleshooter means you can correct problems quickly. If you are consistently having the same problem, a few adjustments can have a major impact on your ability to improve and enjoy the game more. In my own game, I was plagued by shots that flew out to the right, with an occasional duck hook thrown in. By making a few conscious adjustments, I rid myself of a nemesis that had bothered me for years.

We often tend to accept our faults and adjust to them. Many times I would play for my wild hook and hope it would stay in play. We have all played with golfers who have very bad slices. Instead of getting rid of the slice in the first place, they aim to the left and make a wide outside-in swing. In effect, their open stance and swing plane are setting them up to slice. The adjustment is not a cure but an acceptance of a fault. Some golfers have become so ingrained in this self-defeating mode that they find it disturbing to try to line up squarely and take the club back straight.

Making significant improvement involves the willingness to change. It is better to adjust on the practice tee than on the course, because one shot, good or bad, does not indicate real change. But hitting hundreds of balls can eradicate a bad habit. After all, it took years to develop the bad habit, and it will take a lot of swings to train your muscles and develop a feel for the right swing so that the change is incorporated into your golf makeup. At PGA events, I noted how touring pros headed to the practice tee after a favorable round. They would often practice one shot that had given them trouble during the day. Once satisfied that they had cured the fault, they would not hit any other shots for the day.

Apply this method to your own game. To spot a fault, correct it and move on is a system of seeking continuous improvement. As you analyze your game, try to isolate the one fault that consistently occurs. Focus on that fault and remove it. It may be a good idea to make out three-by-five cards, as I did, describing a particular fault and the proper troubleshooting remedies to cure it. I would use the three-by-five cards as little lesson plans during practice and as quick check-ups or reminders during play. The following are some of the most common faults of golf and the troubleshooting actions you can take to cure them.

Slice

Nine out of ten beginners start with a slice or a ball that breaks sharply to the right (assuming you are right-handed). Some move on, correcting this fault and becoming good golfers, while others give in and play with it as part of their game. The sliced shot robs you of both distance and accuracy and severely restricts your options as you approach a hole. If you slice chronically, you do not have to consider it inevitable. With the proper attitude and the right knowledge, you don't have to be a slicer.

A slice results from the clubface opening as it strikes the ball or closing as it cuts outside-in across the ball. Check several points as you troubleshoot this problem:

- *Grip.* Many slicers have a grip in which the left hand is turned too far to the left. Check to see that your left thumb is at the "one o'clock" position on the shaft and the V formed by your left hand points to the right side of your chin. The right-hand thumb should be at the "eleven o'clock" position on the shaft with the V of the right hand also pointing at the right side of your chin. This type of grip gives your wrists and hands the freedom to square themselves to the ball at impact and prevent the clubface opening at impact.

- *Alignment.* If you have been playing a slice for a while, you have probably developed the habit of aiming to the left. This alignment is self-defeating, because it throws the swing plane into an outside-in pattern and causes you to spin the ball laterally. Check to see that your feet, hips and shoulders are all parallel to your target line. But simply aligning yourself will not correct the problem; you must also make a change in your takeaway. When he tries to adjust his takeaway so that it is square to the target line, the slicer is commonly plagued by a perception problem. Because he has swung outside-in for years, everything else seems very awkward to him. The following drill using two coins helped me work on a square takeaway.

Start out by sighting your target from behind the ball. Place one coin six inches in front of the ball and one six inches behind the ball along the target line. With the club square, take your normal stance to see that your feet, hips and shoulders are all parallel to the target line. Slowly move the club back to one coin, pass over the ball and out to the coin in front of the ball. Repeat this drill over and over until you feel that you have gained an understanding of what it looks like to take the club back straight and how the club looks coming square into the ball. Make sure that the clubface is square as well. When you are freely taking the club back squarely, move the coins back and up to about twelve inches. As you turn back in your swing, you will notice that the clubface will start to come inside of your target line naturally. In practice, use the coins to make your target line and to help you bring the clubface back squarely. Never get outside of the line as you hit balls.

- *Downswing.* The most common cause of a slice is casting from the top. Many golfers get to the top of their swings in good shape, but then let their hands act as if they were casting a fly rod. The move from the top is one in which the wrists stay cocked, and the feeling is one of pulling down. By letting your hands go at the top, the clubface is often thrown into an outside-in loop.

As a drill, get yourself into the position at the top of your swing. Without doing anything else, hold your wrists in that position, and with a straight left arm, pull down in one piece until your hands are in front of you. Every time you start down, say to yourself, "pull." Think of pulling a chain.

Hook

The factors that cause the hook are opposite of those which cause the slice. Thus, the system of checks is the same as for the slice, but the corrections are somewhat different:

- *Grip.* Check to see that your right hand is not too much under the shaft. The best way, again, is to make sure that your thumbs and Vs are in the proper position. Sometimes an overly firm grip with the right hand will cause the face to shut. Remember to hold the club with a light grip.

- *Stance.* Players who have trouble with the hook often close their stance severely in order to allow for it. Again, check your alignment to ensure that your feet, hips and shoulders are square to the target line. Use the coin drill to make sure that you are not jerking the clubface inward during the takeaway.

- *Ball Position.* Sometimes a hook is caused by playing the ball too far forward. To correct this, the driver should be hit off your left heel. Take a normal stance with your driver and check to see where you have been placing the ball in your stance. Adjust by moving the ball back in your stance slightly with each shorter club.

- *Casting.* As with the slice, a hook, and usually a "duck-hook," is caused by letting go at the top and throwing the clubface into a loop so that you strike the ball with a sharply closed face. Again, note the drill that emphasizes a pulling down from the top of the swing.

Topped Shot

The topped shot is an extremely frustrating one in which the clubface strikes the top of the ball, sending it a short distance along the ground. In watching players who hit a lot of topped shots per round, I have noticed that they seem to crouch down too low at address. Many players bend their knees and wrists at address so much that they look like they are going to sit down. They come out of the crouch on the backswing, then head back into it on the downswing. I think this bobbing motion, which makes it difficult to control the club, is the cause of most topped shots. The best cure is to stand up straight at address with just a slight break at your knees and a moderate bend at your waist. Keep the head still and turn back, making a full shoulder-turn. Having the ball too far forward in your stance can be another cause. Check your ball position. Finally, many beginners have a tendency to try to scoop the ball into the air by making a lifting movement at impact. Let the club do the work by hitting through the ball.

Shank

The shanked shot is one in which the ball strikes the hosel on the inside part of the clubface. The ball will shoot out almost directly right of the intended flight. This shot is demoralizing and can create a great deal of anxiety; one shank usually indicates more are on the way. Some guys even think they are contagious. We can generally pinpoint two culprits: 1) taking the club to the inside too quickly and then coming back at the ball at a sharp angle from the inside or looping the club from the outside of a square target line; 2) poor balance in which you move onto your toes at impact. Often the shank will occur with a shot that has the ball below your feet.

Cure the shank by being careful during the takeaway, ensuring that the clubface goes straight back from the ball instead of being jerked to the inside. You should set your weight on the insides of your feet and keep your head as still as possible at the center of your hub. The shank is caused simply by moving either your body or the clubface toward the ball from the inside.

Fat Hit

A fat hit occurs when the clubface strikes the ground behind the ball. The causes of this shot have to do with the right side. The fat shot usually occurs when weight is not transferred to the left side as the downswing starts. With the weight still on the right side, the club is thrown down with the hands from the top of the swing, slamming into the ground. To cure this fault, use a swing cue ("slide" is a good one) to remind yourself to make a sliding motion with your hips at the start of the downswing. This action will ensure that you get your weight over to the left side. Another cause, though less common, is simply dropping the right shoulder on the downswing. To correct this, concentrate on pulling down from the top and making the swing cue, "left shoulder under, right shoulder under." This will help you to make a pivot around your head rather than having your shoulders work independently.

Pushed Shot

The pushed shot is a shot that flies to the right of the target. Usually well-hit, it is not the result of a slice or fade. The first thing to check is to make sure that you are aligned properly. Many times, shots that are labeled *pushes* are really the result of lining up to the right of the target. If your alignment is fine, then the shot may indeed be a push. The pushed shot is the result of a blocking action created by failing to turn the hips out of the way. As the downswing comes into the ball, the hips stay closed and force the arms and hands onto a plane that sends the ball out to the right. Sometimes a player will subconsciously compensate by rolling his hands in toward the ball, creating a nasty hook. To correct the pushed shot, open the left foot slightly by turning it toward the target. This turn should help make an easier hip-turn. In practice, you should make a conscious effort to clear the hips out of the way as part of the motion toward impact. By slowing down the tempo of the swing, this kind of adjustment is more easily accomplished and integrated into a swing pattern.

Pulled Shot

The pulled shot is one that flies straight to the left. As with the pushed shot, your alignment should be checked first. The pulled shot is the result of poor footwork or an incomplete backswing. With poor footwork, the golfer makes a swinging movement back to the right side and stays there. In this position, the usual reaction is to open your shoulders and drive the ball to the left. The key to correcting this fault is to do a drill emphasizing proper footwork and tempo. Without a club and with your hands in front of you, rehearse your proper footwork with a one-two-three swing-through, as in a waltz. On "one," lift your left heel as you turn back; on "two," reach the top of the swing with your weight on the right side; and with "three," push off with your right foot and transfer the weight to your left side.

General Wildness

Some days, it seems that nothing is going right. The ball seems to be flying all over the place in no particular pattern. This syndrome can create high scores and destroy confidence. The best time to catch it is in your pre-round practice. But if you are unable to hit balls before you play, you can take corrective action on the course. What I do is call a time-out. I simply get off by myself for a very brief time between shots or while waiting for the foursome in front to play out and run through a brief checklist to remind me of the basics. I consciously review the fundamentals by using the acronym TAGS.

T   Tempo—Slow down and make sure I pull down from the top; no hands

A   Alignment—Square feet, hips and shoulders

G   Grip—Check thumbs and Vs

S   Shoulders—Make a full turn; left shoulder under, right shoulder under

I make a few smooth practice swings, and I am ready to play again with a positive mental attitude. By taking this thirty- to sixty-second break, you can save yourself a day of aggravation. I tell myself that the round is just beginning at that point. The previous bad shots are simply water over the dam.

8

INTO THE CUP

For the high handicapper, the shots mentioned in chapter six are the ones that balloon scores. But once a golfer starts scoring in the 90s or better, the emphasis shifts to proficiency around and on the green. Par golf is structured to allow two putts per hole. So in effect, *one-half* of your total score inevitably comes on or around the green. Regardless of how you play from tee to green, your performance around the green will have at least an equal impact on your score. Playing well can give us much satisfaction, but scoring well is the bottom line.

Putting and chipping have an odd relationship to the rest of the game. I have seen very good golfers who were relatively poor around the green. On the other hand, we have all seen the guy who scrapes it around the course only to be a wizard on the green. For years, I regarded play around the green as mostly a matter of luck. The only time I practiced chipping or putting was while waiting to tee off before a round. Even then, my practice consisted of hitting balls towards the hole with no conscious thought of technique and the mental process required to play the shots properly. Chipping and putting were not as much fun as hitting full shots, and because I was so inept around the green, I avoided the shots as much as possible.

Inept is a kind word to describe how I once played around the green. On a normal day, I would average seven to eight three-putt greens per round. And this figure does not reflect the short putts I missed or the chip shots I stubbed or sent skimming over the green. One time, I stood over a thirty-foot putt while my three playing partners stood ten feet to the right of the cup to watch. I pulled up off the ball and hit a putt that rolled at a forty-five-degree angle. I ended up ten feet behind my partners. Out of courtesy, they just quickly looked at me with puzzled expressions. To break the ice, I simply asked them to please get off my line. While good for a few laughs at the time, I realized that I had to make drastic changes in my short game to become a good golfer.

What I learned from research, study and practice on the short game came as a surprise to me. Technique, for one thing, is critical to good golf play around the greens. In terms of results, it may be even more important than in the full swing. Another facet of the short game that intrigued me is that mastery is much more easily approached than other areas of golf. In the full swing, such problems as lack of coordination or flexibility loom as formidable hindrances. But in the short game, proper technique can readily overcome these flaws. Most importantly, I feel that by acquiring a solid short game you can remove pressure from other areas of your game. For example, on a long par five, I no longer feel compelled to smack an extra-long drive. As I stand on the tee, I know that I can rely on my short game to make up for a short drive or even a missed shot. With a good short-game routine, bogeys will turn into pars and expected pars occasionally turn into birdies.

Chipping

The grip used for chipping is essentially the same as for your other shots. The one thing that I do differently, however, is to grip the club a little more firmly with my left hand (*see figure 20*). The chip shot requires a stroke that is dominated by the left hand, which leads the clubhead back and through the ball. By taking a slightly firmer grip with the left hand, I promote the feeling of controlling the club with my left side instead of becoming wristy. The grip should be soft as a whole, but not so light as to cause a loss of control. I choke down on the grip, depending on the distance, but the hands should be at the bottom of the grip for better control and feel of the clubhead.

To set up for the chip shot, take a stance that is open, with your left foot turned slightly toward the target. With an open stance, you can make a smooth stroke with a minimum of body movement. The weight is slightly onto the left side, the knees flexed comfortably, a bend at the waist and the head centered over the ball. The left arm should be straight (not stiff) so that it creates a straight line from your left shoulder to the clubhead behind the ball. This kind of setup will help you make the kind of stroke that prevents fat shots and eliminates the tendency to scoop at the ball.

The stroke of the chip shot is directly related to the setup. With your left arm straight and wrists firm, the stroke resembles a pendulum. I feel as if my left side is doing all of the work during the stroke. I take the club straight back with the left hand and lead it back through the ball with the left hand. My wrists are not stiff, but they do not break or roll during the stroke. There is no effort to bring the right hand into the ball in a hitting motion.

Like most other high handicappers, my problems in chipping resulted from being too wristy. Inconsistent by nature, the wristy stroke causes many problems. It can result in a fat shot where the club stubs the ground behind the ball or a skulled shot where the clubhead hits the top of the ball. Even when good contact is made, the difficulty in controlling distance with the wrists leads to inconsistency. You will be long one time, then short the next.

figure 20

A Hacker No More

I play the ball toward the front of my stance and about even with my left heel. I try to center my head so that I feel I am looking directly at the back of the ball. While I do not use a real forward press with my full shots, I do use one for chipping. (A forward press is a slight forward movement of the hands or legs as a start for the backward movement of the swing.) As a starting movement for the backswing, I found that the slight movement of my hands toward the hole serves two purposes. First, it breaks the tension in my hands and arms, allowing me to make the short backswing in a smooth, lever-type action rather than in a wristy, jerky motion. Second, it closes the face slightly, promoting a shot that flies low and rolls a good distance. The chip shot is one that should fly low and then roll about three-fourths of the distance to the hole. Too many things can go wrong with a chip that flies too high or long. It is easier to judge roll than it is to judge flight, so my best advice is to get the ball on the ground and rolling toward the cup as soon as possible.

I concentrate on making as little body movement as possible. The left side is the key to making a pendulum-type motion from the left shoulder on down. The head remains still, and there is no need to move it from the action of your shoulders as there is a minimum of turning movement.

This stroke felt somewhat stiff to me at first and almost robot-like in its execution. With practice, however, I became relaxed over the ball and gained confidence in the pendulum motion of the stroke. You should be aware that the change from a wristy stroke to a firm one will indeed feel awkward at first. Stick with it, however, because it pays dividends. After mastering this technique, I can honestly say that I have hit hundreds of chip shots without stubbing the club behind the ball once. With my old, wristy chip stroke, I would stub chip shots several times per round. It is almost impossible to mishit a chip shot using the pendulum motion as long as you keep a straight left side, head still and concentrate on being smooth.

Club Selection. Once you get near the green, the club that you select is dictated by the situation. Too often, the high handicapper will use one favorite club exclusively from 30 yards into the green. This just does not make sense, since the main consideration in making chip shots is the amount of flight and roll required based on the terrain to be negotiated. A basic rule of thumb is to use less loft as you get closer to the green. Some instruction books call for using a 2- or 3-iron from close to the green. I tried using the long irons to chip, but the long shafts are awkward to handle and the lack of loft makes it difficult to judge a landing zone for the ball. My advice is to go with the more lofted clubs that are easier to handle and produce a natural lift. One of my key swing thoughts is to let the club do the work. The more lofted clubs lend themselves to a predictable flight and eliminate any tendency for me to scoop at the ball. The lowest lofted club that I chip with is the 5-iron.

Strategy. For all chips shots, there are several factors that you must consider. The first thing that I do is establish my target line. As with other shots, I get behind the ball, sight along the target line and find a spot two or three feet in front of the ball that will serve as a marker. Because the chip shot involves roll, I know that I must read the slope of the green as if I were making a putt. I also need to calculate the speed and distance based on the green conditions, slope and type of lie. Once I have made these determinations, I select my landing zone. I visualize the shot from start to finish. I imagine the flight of the ball to a particular spot and the amount of bounce and roll required to bring me to the hole. From behind the ball, I select one spot along the target line that I want the ball to land on. I choose a club that will produce the amount of flight required to land on my spot.

When you are over the ball with your target line marked and your landing zone designated, all you have to do is stroke the ball along the target line and land it near your landing zone. You have done all that you can do to hit the perfect shot. The high handicapper tends to think of only the hole in this situation, while the good golfer breaks the shot down into manageable components that make the shot much easier to execute.

Around the green, you are faced with two basic options for getting the ball close to the hole. One is to hit a pitch shot that pops high and then sits down quickly. The other is to hit a basic chip shot that lands quickly and rolls most of the distance to the cup. The choice is determined by the type of terrain that you must traverse. The pitch shot is played with a lofted club such as the pitching or sand wedge, while the chip shot may involve the use of 6- or 7-iron.

One rule of thumb that I always use is to land the ball on the green. A ball that lands on the fairway grass can bounce erratically or have its roll affected by the grass. On the green, bounce and roll are predictable because of the uniform texture of grass and terrain. The only exception to this rule comes when the pin is cut very close to the edge of the green and requires a shot that lands on the apron.

To decide whether to loft a shot and make it stop without much roll or to chip it and have the ball run to the hole, determine the slope and speed of the green that lies along your target line. Generally, if the green slopes downhill from you, it is best to chip just onto the green and let it roll to the cup. It is easier to control roll rather than flight when faced with a downhill shot. On the other hand, if the green slopes uphill to the hole, I prefer to pitch the ball high and land it near the pin. The slope of the green will help the ball stop quickly, so I do not have to worry about roll. For terraced greens, where the pin is on the top level, I find it easier to chip the ball so that it runs up the slope rather than to pitch over the slope and stop the ball on the top level. Trying to bank the ball into the side of the slope is unpredictable, so I tend to stay clear of this technique. For greens that have many undulations and side slopes, it is best to pitch over them if possible.

The ground between you and your landing zone is critical to the type of shot you should play. Shots over bunkers, heavy fringe grass, mounds and depressions require the pitch shot. For this shot, open your stance wide, play the ball well up front in your stance, and hit down and through the ball. Many novice golfers tend to make an almost full swing and let up on the downswing, causing a wide assortment of problems. I take a short backswing and make a firm downswing with a fair amount of wrist action that causes the ball to pop into the air, then set down quickly, much like the lob shot described earlier. The key is to hit down on the ball and follow through in a smooth motion. Let the club do the work of getting the ball into the air.

Judging distance on pitch and chip shots was always a nemesis for me. Too often I would hit a shot that was on line but hopelessly short, ending up 40 feet from the cup. To find out how your ball will react on the green, you need to take into consideration the texture of the green, its slope and speed. If possible, I will walk up onto the green to feel how soft the ground is near my landing zone. This gives me a good idea of how much bounce there will be after the ball lands. I also check to see if the green is wet or dry, fast or slow, and read the break of the green along my target line. I then walk halfway back to my ball and look back and forth along the target line. This perspective gives me a much better feel for the distance than simply standing behind the ball. Sometimes I take a practice swing from the halfway point. When I move back to the ball, I have a better understanding of what it will take to hit the ball twice the distance. As a poor player, distance was a guessing game. I hit and hoped instead of taking charge of the shot to determine distance. From practice, I am now able to calibrate the amount of distance required for each shot by setting my backswing. For all my chip and pitch shots, I use the same type of stance with the same amount of force in the downswing. I set my distance with my backswing. I take a short backswing for a short chip, and I extend the backswing for longer shots. For practice, I have settings for my backswing that will approximate the distance that I need to negotiate. For example, if I have a 20-yard chip, I know how far back I should bring the club to produce that particular distance. This calibration requires experimentation and practice. But once you learn this little trick, all of the guessing will be taken out of your short game.

Before a round, I always hit chips and pitches to the practice green. I do this not so much to practice, as to see how the ball reacts on the green in regard to bounce and roll. I also check to see how the ball comes out of various lies, such as heavy and normal fairway grass, as this may vary from course to course. During the round, watch how the balls of your playing partners react upon hitting the green.

Many golfers have difficulty hitting chips and pitches from sloping lies. For a downhill chip, use a lofted club, play the ball back in your stance, set your weight on your right foot and keep your head still. The stroke should be firm and downward so that the ball pops up from the loft of the club. Do not try to scoop the ball; let the club do the work. For an uphill lie, play the ball up in your stance, weight on your left foot and head still. Let the club follow the slope of the hill and avoid the tendency to pick the ball clean. Use a less lofted club; the hill's slope will cause the ball to fly into the air. When judging distance, remember that the ball will tend to land and sit quickly.

I use the putter off the green in one situation only—there are only a few feet of intervening land, the grass is cut very low and the ground is smooth and firm. Using the putter off the green is often a mistake because of the terrain that has to be traversed to get the ball onto the green. Remember, the less variables involved in bounce and roll, the better. If you can chip over grass and bumpy ground, then by all means take this easier route.

In chipping or pitching, the idea is to get the ball close and in position for an easy putt. Billiard players are often two or three shots ahead of themselves in selecting ball position. The good golfer, too, always considers ball position in chipping or pitching to the hole. The goal is to leave yourself a short, straight putt. Always prefer an uphill putt to a downhill putt, and a right-to-left-breaking putt, as opposed to a left-to-right. When you select your target line for your chip, keep in mind the kind of putt that you want to leave for yourself. For example, if you have a downhill chip, try to go by the cup slightly. If it is on an uphill chip, leave the ball below the hole. Many good players imagine a three-foot ring around the hole as their target area. They know that if they get it in the "washtub," they will be able to make the putt. This approach also serves to remove the pressure of a small target aimed at from a distance. The key is to leave yourself that easy, short putt in order to save a stroke.

If you shoot in the high 90s to high 80s, chances are that you miss a lot of greens. By mastering the chip and pitch shots, you will be able to realize a vast improvement in your scoring in a relatively short period. As your game improves, the chip and pitch shots will serve as the shot that will save a par or make a birdie for you. The attention that you give to these important shots will result in an overall confidence that will carry to the other parts of your game.

Putting

The top players in the world average about 30 putts per round, which roughly translates to about 43 percent of their total score. On the other hand, the high handicapper who shoots near 100 will average about 36 putts or 36 percent of his total score. But these statistics are misleading. The touring pros, who usually hit the green in regulation from long distances out from the hole, have relatively long first putts. The high handicapper usually misses the green and pitches or chips from close range. The high handicapper may have several one-putts as a result of pitching and chipping from close distances. The pros' one-putt opportunities are usually for birdie. The touring pro will have very few three-putt greens, while the high handicapper may average four to six per round. Earlier, I spoke of the special approach shots as the "scoring" shots. For the high handicapper, they are indeed the shots that influence high scores. However, as you improve and develop a solid game from tee to green, putting will become proportionately more important to your total score.

I had always labored under the misconception that putting was a matter of luck. This may be true for the high handicapper. The poor golfer's game does, in fact, rely heavily on luck. Over a 12-foot putt, he will tend to hit the ball in the direction of the hole and hope. But the good golfer sets up with the expectation of making the putt. Good putting is the result of skill and technical knowledge that has been acquired through practice and experience. In my quest to become a good golfer, I made the commitment to take control of my putting and remove the luck factor from this important phase of the game. I have gone from an atrocious putter to a better-than-average one. As I stand over a putt now, I have a genuine feeling of confidence in my stroke and my ability to putt consistently well. The feeling of confidence is not a phony sense of ego but a sincere belief that, if I execute my stroke properly and use the knowledge of putting that I have acquired, I will obtain good results consistently.

The good putter has a consistent stroke that produces a solid hit and predictable roll every time. The confidence comes from knowing that this repeating stroke will not let you down. Although this may sound painfully obvious, I seriously doubt if most golfers who shoot around 100 have a clear idea of the proper putting stroke or the true feeling of confidence that accompanies it. As a high handicapper, I know I did not have a stroke I could depend on for accurate putts.

By becoming a good putter, you will not only realize significant improvement in scoring, but you will create opportunities to employ different strategies as you attack a hole. For example, instead of trying to force a risky shot into a closely guarded pin, the confident putter can lay up short or play to a safe part of the green, knowing that his putting can be trusted. For the good putter, a missed green does not automatically translate into a bogey. In fact, most good players will get the ball down in two shots from around the green three out of five times. With attention to proper technique and practice, the gains in scoring and overall confidence in your putting can be realized in a relatively short period of time.

Selecting a Putter. I have a putter graveyard in my cellar as a testimony to the number of times that I have changed putters. I finally realized that my putting problems came from my putting stroke, not my putter. But a good putter can make a difference in your ability to make a good stroke, and consequently affects your confidence as a putter.

There are, of course, many criteria for selecting a putter, but the foremost one should be that the club feels good to you. Always hit a few putts with a putter before you buy it, because many clubs have different characteristics at impact. Some putters transmit a great deal of feel, while others have very little. The amount of feel that you require is merely a matter of personal choice.

Some other considerations are lie, length, weight, mass and clubhead style. There are literally hundreds of putter styles to choose from in a typical pro shop. Begin by selecting a putter that fits your stance. If you putt from a crouch, for example, you may need a putter that has a short shaft and an upright lie. Putters usually come in three types of lie: flat, standard and upright. If you take your normal stance, the clubhead should lie perfectly flat on the ground. By all means, do not change your putting style to fit the putter.

Many new putters feature heel- and toe-weighting that negates the amount of twisting caused by off-center hits. You should, however, establish the sweet spot or center of your putter and mark it. To do this, hold the club at the grip with your index finger and thumb so that it swings back and forth freely. Tap the clubface with a ball until you find the exact spot that causes the clubhead to swing back perfectly straight and without twisting.

A good putter should also have enough weight and mass to help create a repeatable, consistent stroke. Putters that are very thin or light may be difficult to control at impact. Most top players tend to use putters that are on the heavy side.

The grip should feel comfortable in your hands. I prefer a grip that is thick, with a flattened top to allow the thumbs to be placed straight down the shaft. The clubface should be easy to align. It should help you set up square along the target line. Many new putters, such as *Slotline*,™ have highlighted crosshairs that assist you in producing a square alignment. Find one that feels right in your hands, then trust it to do the job.

Stance. Attitudes about the proper stance for putting are surrounded by a lot of hazy thinking. Most golf instruction tells us to select a stance that is comfortable. Being comfortable is one thing, but being functional is another. As I observed numerous putting styles, I noted that many poor putters have stances that work against them. In my own case, I had an open stance that caused me to cut across the ball. I have seen stances that promote swaying and cause the pushing and pulling of strokes.

In taking a good putting stance, there are several criteria to consider. While there are many schools of thought and many good putters who serve as contradictions, I believe it is in the best interest to start with a square stance. In developing a new putting style, I decided to master the basics first. The putting stance that works best for me is one in which my feet, hips and shoulders are perfectly aligned along the target line. By opening or closing your stance, you have a tendency to push or pull your putts. It takes a good degree of skill to make a square stroke from an off-line stance.

Many players do not know if they are aligned to the left or right of the hole. One way to check to see if you are set up squarely is to line up a straight 25-foot putt. Take your normal stance over the ball, and then lay the club down so that it touches the tips of both shoes. Now go back behind the ball, and check the direction of the club compared to your intended target line.

Another good idea is to get your eyes over the ball so that they create a perpendicular line to the target. This will enable you to make a stroke that goes along the target line. If your head and eyes are back off the ball, you may have a distorted perception of the square stroke. Many players who stand back from the ball have strokes that are very upright, an indication that the clubface is opening and closing along the target line.

The stance should be comfortable; that is, you should feel no tension in any part of your body. There is a caveat, however: you should not become so comfortable that your body is free to move during the stroke. Slight movement of the head or body during the putting stroke can result in the putt straying well off-line. The stance, then, should emphasize good balance and some kind of mechanism that will hold the body still throughout the stroke (*see figure 21*). Arnold Palmer uses a pigeon-toed stance that prevents swaying. Other mechanisms used to hold the body still include taking a knock-kneed stance, crouching very low, spreading the width of the stance and standing stiff-legged. I prefer a shoulder width stance with my weight slightly on the left side. As the distance of the putt grows shorter, my stance grows narrower. There is no weight shift during the putting stroke, so you should feel compact, with very few moving parts. I toe-in with my feet to get the feeling that I am locked into a solid stance. I play the ball just inside my left heel for all putts to promote one consistent stroke.

There are two schools of thought on the position of the arms in the stance. Some prefer to keep the arms in close to the body; others place the arms away from the body and point the left elbow at the hole. You should choose the arm position that makes the putting stroke comfortable, because neither style offers any particular advantage over the other. I prefer my arms in close to my body with my wrists high, as it gives me a feeling of being compact and offers me a sense of control for creating a repeating stroke.

The Grip. The putting grip relates directly to the stroke. Basically, you stroke a putt by either putting with your wrists or putting with your arms and shoulders. A wrist putter prefers a grip that offers the wrists the freedom to act as a hinge. For the arm-and-shoulder putter, the wrists need to be de-emphasized, and the hands become a one-piece unit.

For the wrist putter, the basic interlocking, overlapping and ten-finger grips produce a free movement of the wrists during the putting stroke. The one grip that seems to be most popular among wrist putters is the ten-finger or baseball grip. Many players using this grip split their hands so that there is a gap of one-half inch up to several inches. With this grip the left hand acts as a base for holding the club while the right hand does the work of making the stroke.

One element common to all good putting grips is that both thumbs run down under the center of the shaft. In taking a full swing, we must turn the clubface in our hands in order to bring it back and forth in a long arc. With the putter, however, our goal is to minimize the amount of turn in the

figure 21

Into the Cup

clubface. Running your thumbs down the center of the shaft restricts your wrists from rolling and prevents the opening and closing of the clubface during the stroke. You may have noticed that many putters come with grips that are flattened on top in order to assist the placement of the thumbs.

For years, I was a wrist putter with very poor results. There are many fine wrist putters, but for me the wrist stroke was too unpredictable and too difficult to repeat successfully. I opted for a grip and stroke that took the wrists out of the movement. Putting with the wrists requires a great deal of skill. With the hands working against each other, it is difficult to control distance by striking the ball with the right hand. I also found the wrist stroke difficult to maintain from round to round. By using a stroke controlled by my arms and shoulders, I am able to make a solid repeating motion. The bigger the muscles, the easier it is to create a consistent movement. Swing your arm freely in front of you, using the large muscles of your shoulder and upper arm. The arm-swing will repeat the same arc time after time. Now, hold your arm out and snap your wrist back and forth in a pendulum motion. If you look carefully, you will see that your hand makes different arcs. When I changed my putting style, I wanted a good basic stroke that I could count on every time. The gross motor skills are more reliable than the fine motor skills for producing a reliable motion.

In order to develop a grip that would de-emphasize the wrists, I studied the top arm-and-shoulder putters. Jack Nicklaus, Corey Pavin and other top players place their left index finger in the notch between the second and third fingers of their right hand. This grip provides a feeling of the hands working as a unit. It is called the reverse overlap. Using this grip, I was able to move the club in a very smooth, comfortable manner. With this grip your hands feel like a one-piece unit that moves the clubhead in unison with the movement of the arms and shoulders.

With the clubface on the ground, I grip the putter with my right hand. Making sure that the clubface is square to the target line, I slide my left hand onto the club and move my left index finger over the top of the fingers of my right hand. I make sure that my thumbs run directly down the shaft. I continually check my grip during a round by bringing my wrists close together. I find that this little check is helpful, because it is easy to slip into the habit of moving your hands under the shaft and turning your thumbs outward from the middle. I have incorporated the check into my pre-putt routine.

The putter should be gripped with light pressure. At no time are the muscles of the hands or forearms tensed. You should apply only enough pressure so that you control the club during the stroke and impact. Firm pressure translates into a jerky stroke and inconsistent control of speed and distance. If you have ever hit a putt much harder than you wanted or expected, chances are your grip pressure was much too strong. To guard against this, especially on tricky putts, I remind myself to grip the club lightly by saying "soft hands."

The Stroke. While driving home from a PGA Tour event, I tried to think of one thing about the pros' game that surprised me the most. It was not the great drives or the smooth tempo of their swings. The one thing that appeared radically different from the average club golfer's game was the putting stroke. While certainly not as exciting as the swing with a driver, the pros' putting strokes seemed substantially different from what I had seen on any local course.

I am thoroughly convinced that more putts are missed because they are mishit than for any other reason. One thing that always sets my head shaking is to play with a guy who seems to take forever to line up a putt. He will look at it from every angle known to man, lie down behind it and plumb-bob his putter. He finally will get up to the ball and make a stroke that cuts the ball so badly that it has absolutely no chance from the start. I think this guy would improve 100 percent if he spent just half the time lining up the putt and devoting the other half to concentrating on his stroke.

A good putting stroke is one that stays along the target line, strikes the ball solidly and is repeatable. I concentrate on the putting stroke by looking at the back of the ball. With my head over the ball, I am able to get a definite sense of the target line. I use a very slight forward press in which I move my hands toward the target ever so slightly just before starting the back-swing. I have the feeling that my left hand is taking the putter back from the ball. The backswing is low and slow and comes straight back along the target line. On the downstroke, there is no breaking of the wrists but a swinging motion of the arms and shoulders that brings the clubface square to the ball and through along the target line with the clubhead remaining as low to the ground as possible (*see figures 22a, b, c*). The clubhead moves through the ball smoothly, striking it solidly. Golfers who stop the club at impact are actually slowing the momentum of the club before impact takes place. This kind of a movement produces a jerky stroke that throws the clubface off a square alignment.

The proper strike of the ball should send it along the target line immediately. Check to make sure that you are not catching the ball on the downswing or upswing. If you are striking the ball in either fashion, the ball will pop into the air for a short distance, then bounce before it begins its roll. These bounces cause the ball to stray off-line. If you are popping

figure 22a

figure 22b

the ball instead of rolling it, it will be obvious on your long putts. In practice, check how your ball is reacting just after impact. Make adjustments in your ball position so that you catch the ball at the low point of your stroke. The key is to have the putter remain just above the ground as it comes into the ball and stay along the target line for as long as possible after the ball is struck.

The great destroyer of a sound putting stroke is head or body movement. I suspect that many poor putters are not aware that they move their heads during the stroke. I have seen golfers who actually follow the clubhead back with their eyes and head. On the follow-through, many golfers again let their heads trace the movement of the clubhead. One way of checking to see if you move your head during the stroke is to tape a string onto the bill of a cap. The string should touch the floor when you take your normal putting stance. Now, stroke the ball in your normal manner and see if the string moves during the stroke. This is a great practice technique as well for putting on a carpet at home. Don't try to explain it to your family—they just won't understand!

Probably the best tip that I ever received was to avoid looking at the putt at all. Many top players use this as a practice technique, but I use it on the course to make sure that I have absolutely no head movement. After you have struck the ball, there is nothing that you can do to change things, so why not do everything possible *while* you are stroking

figure 22c

the ball? I found that all my head movement problems were solved by this technique.

Getting a Line. Being able to read a green properly serves two purposes. First, you are able to determine the path that your ball should take to the hole; second, the knowledge that you have a fixed line bolsters your confidence for making a solid stroke. Getting a line involves determining what physical elements will affect the roll of the ball and making a visualization of the path it will take.

First I consider the slope of the green. As I approach a green, I take a good look at the big picture. The surrounding terrain will often give clues to subtle breaks on the green. For example, if there is a steep slope next to a seemingly level green, chances are that water will drain away from the slope across the green, creating a grain pattern and subtle slope that will influence the path of the putt. I always look for signs of where water has collected or run off the green, which can give me a clear idea of undulations and slopes that are not readily apparent. I approach my putt from the side at approximately the halfway point. By looking at the putt from the side, instead of standing behind the ball, I not only gain perspective on the terrain of the green but also a better idea of the distance. I then move behind the ball and trace my eyes over the path the ball should take. Remember, there are two things that will cause the ball to break—slope and grain. The slower a ball is traveling, the greater the effect of slope. In other words, a slope near the ball will not affect the path as much as a slope near the hole. Some players use a plumb-bob method, holding the putter perpendicular along the line to the hole.

Grain flow refers to how the grass lies down and points on the green. If the grain is with you, the grass will appear light and shiny. If the grain is against you, it will appear dark and dull. A grain causes your ball to move in the direction in which it is pointing. A grain against you tends to slow your ball down. A strong grain of thick, uniformly bent grass can have a substantial effect on the break of your putt.

Once I have determined the path my ball will take to the hole, I select a spot about three feet from the ball that lies along the target line. My whole philosophy of putting is based on the principle that, if you can make a three-foot putt, you can make a 30-footer. Once I have established the three-foot spot as my intermediate target and have a good sense of distance, I simply try to stroke the ball over the spot. Trying to make a three-footer instead of a 30-footer reduces the margin of error and takes a great deal of pressure off. My main concern is to strike the ball solidly and roll it over my spot with the proper amount of speed to carry it to the hole.

Judging distance had always been a problem for me. Most of my three-putt greens were the result of being woefully long or short on my first putt. I needed to develop a system that would produce consistent results. Developing "touch" seemed too nebulous, involving too many factors that could not be measured. I noted that the touring pros made very consistent strokes for all putts. The only discernible difference for accommodating for distance was an increase in the length of the backswing. By regulating the length of the backswing and equating that length to specific distance, the length of putts can be produced in a consistent system.

Touring pros seldom take full practice swings from tee to green, as they know very well what their swings look and feel like. On the green, however, the pros usually take several practice strokes before putting. These practice strokes are really rehearsal strokes in which they are setting the proper amount of backswing to correlate to the distance of the putt. Before a round, top players will hit putts of varying lengths and make mental notes as to how much backswing is needed to hit putts a specific distance. They establish backswing lengths for 10-, 15-, 20- and 25-foot putts. During actual play, the rehearsal stroke checks how far they should bring the club back. Once they get their setting, they are ready to putt.

To break this method down even further, I walk up to the halfway point of a long putt and take a practice stroke. When I get back to the ball, I then calculate what I must add to the backswing based on what was required from half the distance. This is a very simple but effective method of judging distance that has enabled me to gain a concrete feeling of how I should stroke the ball. In effect, I take the guesswork out of distance and do not have to rely on "touch."

Once over the ball, I know that I have my target line set up; all I have to do is hit a spot that is three feet away. From my rehearsal stroke, I have already programmed the length of the stroke. My only concern, then, is to stay still and make a solid hit on the ball. I feel confident knowing that, if I do my part by striking the ball solidly, I have stacked the deck on my side for a good putt.

Thinking on the Green. Good putters are good thinkers. My improvement as a putter was only partially attributable to my changes in stance, grip and stroke. I also approach each green with a system that allows for sound thinking. On the green, I go into a learning mode in order to determine every possible factor that will affect the roll of the ball. In addition to observing slope, contour and grain, I watch the putts of my playing partners with special interest. In particular, I study how the ball breaks near the hole, regardless of the direction of the putt. The break near the cup is usually the critical part of the putt, and hidden breaks become evident.

I look at the cup itself for information. If the rim of the cup is firm and sharp, I know that I can be slightly more firm with my putt, as the ball will drop sharply at the cup. On the other hand, if the rim is worn or broken, I know that it is best to have the ball die at the hole, because a firm put will spin off of a worn cup.

In choosing my target line, I select a point at which my ball will enter the cup. Using the clock method where "twelve o'clock" is the direct top of the cup, I choose a point such as "four o'clock" as the point that my ball will enter the cup. By focusing on one small point as my target, I create a window for error in which a slight miscalculation may still bring the ball in at "three" or "five o'clock." Using the entire hole as a target creates a wide target line and increases the margin of error.

From behind the ball, as I sight down the target line, I visualize the ball rolling along the line and dropping into the cup. If something does not look right during the visualization—too much break, for example—I rethink the line and start over. I visualize the putt again when I make my rehearsal strokes. Once I have fixed the putt in my mind, I step up to the ball, stroke it and listen for the ball to drop.

To promote consistency, it is important to follow a set routine every time you step onto a green. I use the following system:

- *Approach.* Get the big picture of the layout of the green. Walk up to your putt at the halfway mark to check distance and make a rehearsal stroke.

- *Behind the Ball.* Sight down the target line, visualize the roll of the ball and select the three-foot spot to mark the line.

- *At the Ball.* Make two rehearsal strokes, setting the backswing length to match the distance. Visualize the putt dropping to create confidence.

- *Take Stance.* Make checks to ensure a light grip and a square stance to your three-foot spot.

- *Stroke.* Stroke the ball solidly to the three-foot spot. Keep the head still and listen for the ball to drop.

This routine is efficient and effective. Because you have a clear idea of every step, there is no need to have a debate with yourself over the putt. As long as you pay attention to the three elements of line, distance and stroke, you will have covered all of your bases.

Length

The length of the putt has a direct effect on my overall strategy. For putts of three feet or under, my main thought is to strike the ball firmly toward the center of the hole unless there is a severe break. I use the firm stroke in this situation for several reasons. One, there are usually a lot of spike marks around the hole, and a ball that is moving slowly will be affected by the marks much more than a ball that is rolling quickly. Second, for putts of three feet or under, it does not make sense to me to fool around with break. It is much easier to stroke the ball on a straight line to the cup than it is to rely on a break that may or may not be there.

For putts up to 30 feet, I set my mind on making the putt every time. Many high handicappers simply try to get the ball close and are content to lag the ball to the vicinity of the hole. By trying to make the putt, you cut down your margin of error. Chances are, if you miss the putt but have done all your homework, the remaining putt will be very easy to make. By trying to and expecting to make these medium-range putts, you will find that more and more of these putts will begin to fall.

On putts from a distance beyond 30 feet, my main concern is to get down in two. Avoiding the three-putt green consistently will substantially improve scoring. In this situation, I use the old technique of imagining a three-foot ring around the hole. My target line and distance-setting for my backswing are designed so that the ball will end up inside the three-foot ring. By imagining such a large target, I take the pressure off myself to get the ball close to the hole from a long distance out. For long putts, I will stand a little more erect in order to make a longer backswing. I always think in terms of the putt that will remain to finish the hole.

Practice. Practice is what really builds confidence and consistency in putting. We have all heard about golfers who are streak putters, but the streak begins on the practice green, not on the course. There are two types of putting practice that are essential to building a solid game on the green: pre-round practice and developmental practice.

Before a round, I have three objectives in practice putting:

- To create a feel of a good, solid stroke

- To gauge distance from the greens on that particular day

- To gain confidence in my stroke

I begin by hitting two-foot putts until I am virtually making every one. Doing this develops a smooth stroke that brings the clubhead back and through the ball in a straight line. By having the ball drop into the cup over and over, I build a sense of confidence in my putting stroke. I then move back to three feet and concentrate on stance, grip and keeping my head still. I try to make as many putts in a row as possible and keep track of the count. If I miss, I start over. When I first started this drill, I would usually make four or five putts in a row. Now, I can make between fifteen and twenty on most days before I miss one. This drill is very important as my whole approach to putting is based on being able to make a three-foot putt.

When I am confident that I can make a three-foot putt at will, I move back to about ten feet. I will place balls around the hole at this distance in order to force myself to think over each putt. I sight down the target line and set up as I would for a putt during actual play. I have seen high handicappers hit putts on the practice green in machine-gun fashion. Every putt should have meaning because learning is taking place. I check my grip, stance and stroke with every putt.

I move back progressively to 20 and 30 feet to check my backswing for the proper setting. I then move back to about 40 feet to practice hitting the three-foot ring. Finally, I place a tee in the ground three feet from the ball and stroke it to the tee to simulate my three-foot spot along the target line. The tee also serves to promote confidence—the hole becomes a large target once you step onto the course.

When I set out to practice putting, I always have an agenda set. This is what I mean by developmental practice. I found that I wasted time and did not get much accomplished if I just spent time putting with nothing specific in mind. I always start my practice with the three-foot drills. The type of putt that I practice relates directly to either the kind of greens I will be playing on or on a particular putt that is giving me trouble. For example, if I am going to play a course that has hilly greens, I concentrate on uphill and downhill putts. I pay particular attention to having my stroke match the slope of the hill. I also practice putts that will break left or right. I concentrate on maintaining balance or keeping a stroke that moves through the ball in a straight line. If I have recently had some three-putt greens, I hit putts from 40 feet and follow them up by putting out each ball. I practice a particular putt until I have reached a good level of confidence. I finish all practice putting sessions with my three-foot drills. To practice a specific putt, write down what you want to practice and some key points to remember. Some particular putts that I work on in practice are:

- Uphill

- Downhill

- Break to left/right

- Short putts

- Long putts to three-foot circle

- Putts from the apron

- Putts on terraced greens

- Putt to a dime or tee

- Putts around the clock

- Putt with eyes closed

- Putts to points on cup

Whatever the drill or game you select for use in practice, never hit a putt without concentration. If you do not concentrate on every putt, no real learning or growth takes place. During the off-season, I putt on a carpet with only stance, grip and stroke as my checkpoints, as the carpet does not have the true characteristics of a green. You will make significant progress with practice. Keep track of the number of putts you are averaging per round as well as the amount of time that you spend practicing putting. You should see an inverse relationship between the two—as the amount of practice time increases, the amount of putts decreases.

9

PRACTICE
PRACTICE
PRACTICE

Over the past two years, I have spent a great deal of time on practice tees. I have experimented with a wide range of practice techniques and gradually developed a routine and approach to practice that has been beneficial to my game. I have also spent a great deal of time studying the techniques and patterns of golfers at all levels. I would often strike up conversations with very good golfers to pick their brains about their approach to practice. I looked at every practice session as a learning experience in which I not only worked on my game but gathered as much information as possible on how to make practice pay off on the course.

A principle all good golfers seem to share is to practice with a purpose—always. I think many golfers go to a practice area or driving range with no clear idea of what they are trying to do. Many equate improvement with the quantity of balls hit. As a poor golfer, I would often go to a driving range and blast balls with my driver until I was tired and sore. Afterward, I really had gained no knowledge nor insight, so I made no real improvement in my game. When I made the commitment to become a very good golfer, I decided to look upon practice as my classroom.

As a teacher, I would never consider teaching a semester's work or even presenting one lesson without planning and preparation. Learning, whether it be the multiplication of fractions or the golf swing itself, is too complex a process to be accomplished haphazardly. I devised a curriculum for structuring practice so that it would be comprehensive. It is a blueprint of the scope and sequence of what needs to be learned. It includes not only those topics or areas that need to be addressed, but also the means for learning these topics. I wrote this curriculum in the same way I would approve a curriculum in the field of education.

Set Goals

A goal is where you want to be when you have finished learning. As a golfer, you should set realistic goals that you know are attainable. For example, if you shoot in the high 90s or have a 25 handicap, you may set a goal of consistently breaking 90 or reducing your handicap to 18 in one season. Your goal should be compatible with your commitment. Chopping seven strokes off your handicap in one year will not become a reality unless you also decide to set aside time for practice on a regular basis. Setting a goal is not just an academic exercise. It is the way you eventually measure your progress. Your goal should be in your mind every time you set out to practice. Instead of beating balls, you will have a long-range target to shoot at. Everything you do in practice should be designed to bring you one step closer to that goal.

Self Evaluation

One of the most common questions about improving the game of golf is "Where do I start?" Like the pretest teachers give in school, which enables the teacher to get a starting point and gain an idea of individual strengths and weaknesses, the golfer needs to seek improvement by making a careful analysis of his last five rounds. Pinpoint your areas of weakness and ask yourself why you are having problems in each area. For example, count the number of times you have missed the fairway on your tee shot, the number of greens missed with short irons or the number of putts taken per round. Do you miss the fairways because of a slice? Are your putts missing the hole to the right? By taking a careful inventory of your game, you establish those areas causing high scores. These are the areas that you need to attack first. Building a solid, all-purpose swing is one objective to overall good golf. Narrowing your focus onto your weakest point and turning it into a strength will produce rapid and significant improvement in your game.

Here is a checklist you can use to focus your practice. You may want to add other topics as they apply to your game.

Full Swing	Short Game	Special Shots
Driver	Pitching wedge	Sand shots
Fairway woods	Sand wedge	Uphill
Long irons	Chipping	Downhill
Mid irons	Putting	Sidehill
Short irons	Half shots	Ball above feet
	Pitch and run	Ball below feet
	Lob/cut	Rough
		Hard pan
		Punch
		Fade
		Draw
		Wind
		High shot
		Low shot

The checklist should serve to give you both scope and sequence. Sequence your approach to practice by focusing in on your weak points first. If you need to develop a solid full swing, then begin with the short irons and work your way up to the driver. If your short game is unacceptable, plan a good deal of practice in this area in addition to some with the full swing. For the scope of your practice, use the checklist to make sure that you practice every aspect of the game. To avoid downhill shots because they are difficult and not much fun is to concede to a weakness that is impacting on your overall game. Make sure to develop a plan where you will systematically learn every shot required to become the good golfer that you want to be.

Practice and Learning

It is important to see how practice can be translated into real learning. As I said earlier, educators realize that the learning takes place in three domains: cognitive, affective and psychomotor. Cognitive learning involves the knowledge necessary to acquire a skill or understanding. Most of the preceding chapters of this book dealt with the cognitive aspects of the how-to of making a proper swing or hitting a particular shot. A knowledge and understanding of these skills is essential to becoming a good golfer. Knowing how to make a proper backswing is an essential building block for learning that cannot be overlooked. Many players go through the golfing basics without gaining proper knowledge or instruction of just what they are trying to do on a golf course. In my own case, I never read an instruction book or watched an instructional film on golf once I was out of my teens until I decided to relearn the game.

The affective domain deals with the attitudinal or psychological change that we bring about through learning. In order to be a complete learner and an accomplished golfer, your attitude and mental approach to the game must also be changed. Your attitude towards learning, practice and self-evaluation must be different; it must be more important in your approach to the game than ever before. The fact that you are reading this book means you want to change your golf game. The affective domain also encompasses your emotional stability on the course, your strategic ability and your sense of self-concept as it relates to golf. In the next chapter, we will deal with the mental aspects of the game.

The psychomotor domain refers to the relationship of your mind to your body. For the golfer, it involves making a swing based on verbal and physical cues that tell us how to make the proper moves. For example, in discussing the full swing, we spoke about hitting a spot at the top of the swing. By assuming this spot or position and checking in the mirror, we learn how it feels to be in the proper position and what it looks like when we do it.

As we make a full swing, our objective is to get to that position every time. Our mind develops a sense of what is correct, and our body gives us the feel of what is correct when we execute it properly. Having become aware of what a proper swing feels and looks like, we are able to spot flaws and make adjustments. Without this psychomotor relationship between mind and body, we would be just guessing what is correct or incorrect in the swing. The psychomotor domain is only part of the whole of learning and is driven by the other two domains of cognitive and affective learning.

Practice with a Purpose

Golfers of different ability levels practice in dramatically different ways. The high handicapper tends to use the same club, usually a driver, throughout his practice session. He hits balls in rapid fire sequence. There is no conscious attempt to work on a particular part of the swing, no attention to detail. On the other hand, the pros and low handicappers are very deliberate in practice. They pause after each shot and reflect on what has transpired. The good golfers hit a variety of shots; they work on wedge and half shots as much as they do with the driver. The essential difference is that the good golfer approaches the practice tee as a workshop, a place to learn and grow, while the high handicapper is there mostly for exercise.

I made up my mind to hit every shot in practice with the same intensity that I would bring to a shot during actual play. I line up every shot to a target, choose a spot along the target line, check my grip, stance and alignment. I am not only practicing my swing, I am developing a pattern of setting up properly, aligning myself and checking the components of my setup over and over. Sloppy practice translates into sloppy play. If I catch myself raking over a few balls and hitting them downrange without any conscious thought, I know that it is time for a break. I will go get a soft drink and watch others until I am ready to get back to practicing properly.

Before I set out for the practice tee, I make out a lesson plan on a three-by-five card. This card focuses on the thing I want to work on that day. I found that by selecting one small phase of the game at a time, rather than trying to do too many things, I can reach mastery at a much faster rate. My three-by-five card contains the aspect of the game that I will be working on, as well as the swing cues and checkpoints that will produce the desired swing or movements. A sample card might be as follows:

Long irons
—Sweep the ball

—Play ball off left instep

—Takeaway—low and slow

—Left shoulder under, right shoulder under

—Pull down from the top

The card helps me to stay focused on my practice goals and to avoid getting into the rut of blasting balls with no purpose. Every time I swing, I say the swing cues to myself so that they become second nature to me. On the course, I may only need to have my body make the cues as I swing, because they have been ingrained into my mind from practice.

Depending on your ability level, you may want to guard against overloading yourself. For example, if you only want to work on your drive during practice, then focus on improving one aspect of your full swing with the driver. You may write down "driver," then "takeaway—low and slow." By doing this, you break the swing down and work on perfecting one aspect, in this case, the takeaway. Every time you take the club back, think "low and slow." Work on this until you are satisfied that you have reached your mastery. At your next practice session, work on hitting your spots. On the next, focus on the pull-down motion from the top. Little by little, you will put the components together, but be patient as the change is gradual. Bad shots will reduce as good shots appear with greater regularity. This change, of course, will come over time and is directly related to the amount and quality of practice you undertake.

After each shot, I stop and reflect on what has happened. If it was a good shot, I will savor the moment and try to remember just what that swing felt like so that I can make it repeatable. If I hit a bad shot, I make a slow practice swing to erase it and go back over my swing cues to correct the fault. I note shot patterns to pick up any flaws that might be developing into habits. For example, if my shots consistently land to the right of the target, I know that I should check my stance, alignment and clubface to see what is causing the problem. I guard against overloading myself with corrections. If I am having a day where I'm just not swinging well at all, I will forget it for the day and practice chipping and putting, or simply go home. To practice when everything is going poorly, or when you are tired, only reinforces bad habits.

As you start a practice routine, it is best to proceed slowly. Begin by limiting yourself to twenty-five or thirty-five balls and work up from these gradually. If you become tired or sore from overdoing it on the first few times out, your mind will set up an avoidance to practice. Space out the intervals between shots, take breaks, talk to fellow golfers and enjoy the scenery. Practice should be fun, not drudgery. Learning is always enhanced if the learner has a high interest and satisfaction level. Your attention span and your ability to learn are at their peaks when you are fresh and alert. I never look at practice as work or drill. Rather, I look at it as having the same elements of enjoyment as actual play. There are many days, in fact, that I would rather practice than play. For one thing, I get to hit more shots than

I would playing a round, and I get immediate feedback on changes that produce improvement. Start each practice by stretching and then swinging rhythmically. Hit wedge and 9-irons when concentrating only on rhythm and tempo.

Practice Games

In order to make practice interesting and challenging, I have devised little games and situations to use on the practice tee. If I am practicing lob or cut shots to a green, I imagine there is a high bunker right in front of me that I must get over by popping the ball up high. When practicing with a driver, I try to hit five shots each on the right, center and left of the fairway.

If I have had problems on a particular hole of my course, I will replay the hole from tee to green on the practice tee. One of my favorite games is to play a round of golf by imagining each hole of my course and playing each shot as I would in actual play. I usually play this game at the end of the practice round as a little test of my game. Play every shot as you would on your course by estimating where your shots land. This will give you practice in club selection, strategy and visualization, as well as practice with your swing. If possible, give yourself bad lies, including downhill, sidehill and shots from the rough. A scorecard from your course may help you visualize each hole for terrain and distance.

Sometimes I use little training cards to help me work on some aspect of the game. I will use coins or string to mark my target line in front of and behind the ball. This helps me to check my takeaway and the movement of the clubhead through impact. For chipping practice, I place a coin on the green as a target for where I want to land the ball. I have rubbed my practice balls with a carpenter's chalkball to check where the ball is striking on my irons. All these little gimmicks are ways of making my practice time more interesting and productive.

Pre-round Practice

Before playing, it is to your advantage to practice. The purpose of the pre-round practice is simple: you warm up and get the feel of your swing for that day. After stretching and slowly swinging the heavy clubs, begin by hitting short pitch shots with a wedge. This will help you build rhythm and tempo and give you a sense of making impact with the ball. Concentrate on hitting a crisp shot that strikes the ball first and then takes turf. Gradually increase the length of the shots with the wedge until you are hitting full shots of about 100 yards or so. Move up through your irons, starting with the 9-iron and progressing to the long irons. Move up to the fairway woods, then onto the driver.

Finish by hitting some soft wedge shots to bring back that feeling of tempo and rhythm. Only hit a few shots per club until you are confident with your swing. Practice your pre-shot routine of lining up along your target line and check grip, stance and alignment with every shot. This will help you get the proper mental framework for your round. As mentioned earlier, practice putting and chipping to develop confidence in your short game.

If you can find a time when your course is not used very much, say early evening or a weekday, or early in the morning, you might get out for some worthwhile practice on the course. Go out to the hole that gives you the most problems and play five or six balls from the tee. Try to place your driver in various locations, and your approach shots into various pin placements. By playing the hole that bothers you the most, you will find strategies in attacking it, as well as developing confidence in your ability to play the hole well. You will get a better idea of yardage and the reaction of your ball on the green. This will also help your overall strategy as you approach your nemesis.

Taking a Lesson

Every golfer from hacker to pro can benefit from the instruction of a professional. Many touring pros have teaching pros whom they rely on to help them recover from slumps or correct a problem. The key to taking a lesson properly is to be a good listener. If you do not understand what the pro is trying to tell you, by all means ask questions and have him or her demonstrate. When the pro looks at your swing, make your normal swing. Many times, pros find that golfers try to make super swings, to crush the ball. The pro wants to see the swing you use on the course so he or she can help you. Most pros take a great deal of pride in their ability to help people improve. The golfer has the responsibility to listen, absorb and incorporate the lessons into his practice routine.

Putting and chipping should make up about one-third to one-half of your total practice time to reflect their importance on the course. The total amount of time you spend practicing is an individual decision based on the time restrictions of your daily life. As I made significant gains in my own game, I found myself practicing more than playing. On some days, you may make the choice of practice or play, depending on how you feel about your golf game's improvement. The main point to remember is to practice with a purpose; think of it as learning and make it fun. Your past evaluation will come in the form of lower scores on the course.

A Hacker No More

10

THE MENTAL SIDE

We always hear the cliché "Golf is 90 percent mental" from analysts and instructors of the game. I am not sure that the game of golf can be separated into percentages of the mental and physical. The two components are so intertwined they are indistinguishable. The golf swing itself is a product of both conscious and unconscious thought. Club selection and shot strategy are examples of conscious thought, while reaction to a bad shot, tension and negative input are examples of subconscious thought.

The good golfer has a strong sense of awareness. Technically proficient, he knows what distance each club will produce, what kind of shot will work best and how to compensate for the wind. The good golfer's technical knowledge has helped him build a solid swing and make adjustments when necessary. Yet he also has an awareness of his temperament, emotions and reactions. He knows when tension creeps into his game and when anxiety is being produced from negative thinking. His concentration is focused, and everything he does on the course is designed to maximize his potential.

Many of these things are intangible, difficult to measure and quantify. Yet these intangibles are truly the basis for learning and significant improvement in golf. While I remade my swing and learned the technical aspects of the game, real improvement did not come until I developed sound thinking and self-awareness.

The Mind-Swing Relationship

I asked many good golfers, both pro and amateur, what they thought about during the swing. The answer to this question was almost always: "Nothing." To good golfers, the swing is a matter of feel. The mind senses rhythm, tempo and position, and provides direction and feedback to the body. It is for this reason I used my *shot* method with a mirror to learn the proper swing. By getting into the proper position and checking it in a mirror, I gained a sense of how it felt to get into a proper swing position. As I practiced, I sought this feeling when I swung the club to these spots. Learning how a good swing feels is something that cannot be accomplished with a printed word or picture. By placing your body in the proper positions, whether it be the grip, stance or top of the swing, you gain a sense of feel that can be stored in your mind. With practice, your mind takes over and controls your movements, replicating the feel of a good swing.

A concert violinist does not consciously think about moving his or her fingers from fret to fret while moving the bow with the other hand. The violinist plays by feel, with a sense of what has to be done but with no thought of "little finger to fourth fret." The high handicapper, however, will often overload his mind by consciously trying to orchestrate the swing. Some of the worst swings possible are produced by golfers taking lessons. Instead of feeling the change that the pro is trying to get across, they try to manipulate the change consciously. On the course, your swing should reflect the trust you place in it. The trust is developed from practice and the experience of past success.

I have a rule of never talking about the technical aspects of the swing on the course. Many times a fellow player will ask me to look at his swing, hand position or grip. I politely decline until after the round is completed, because I do not want to cloud my mind with technical thoughts. I rely on how my swing feels to me and make no effort to think of such things as when my hands release. The practice tee is the place for swing development and experimentation. For one thing, no one tip or word of advice would be of any use without repeated practice to incorporate it into your swing. There are no quick fixes for the golf swing. The relationship of movements in the swing is so complex that every productive change has to be brought about with the repetition that builds muscle memory.

Visualization

Top athletes often talk about the importance of visualizing to performance. When a hitter in baseball is said to be "looking curveball," he is doing more than just expecting that pitch. Instead, he actually visualizes the pitcher in his delivery and imagines the pitcher's wrist snapping and the ball spinning as it travels toward the plate. Visualizing is like having a practice pitch or a rehearsal before stepping into the batter's box.

Top golfers use visualization in many ways on the course and in practice. I have incorporated visualization into every aspect of my golf game with good results. As I stand behind the ball to get a target line, I visualize the kind of shot that I want to make. I see the ball rise, fly toward the green, bounce and roll to the pin. Doing this gives me a sense of how the shot should be hit and how the ball will react when it lands. Sometimes, because of visualization, I change the type of shot that I am considering. For example, I visualize a 3-iron shot flying over a trap and sitting quickly on the green. I realize that, in reality, I would not be able to make the shot. I make adjustments based on a realistic appraisal of my own capabilities. From practice, I gain a realistic idea of what I can do with each club.

As I take a slow practice swing before I address the ball, I visualize a smooth, full swing like the one I intend to make over the ball. Through this visualization, I gain a sense of what my swing and shot should look like.

This form of visualization is actually a means of programming yourself for success. You are training your mind to sense the good swing and building an expectation level for a good shot based on reality.

Developing the ability to visualize is a matter of practice. While working for my doctorate at Boston College, I had the opportunity to study under a Jesuit priest named Father Donahue. Father Donahue trained graduate students to think at a higher level than they had been used to or comfortable with in the past. He began by having us visualize our front doors and gradually led us through an exercise that brought us to solving complex organizational issues through visualization. We were trained to imagine the people, places, communication and interaction that would result from a visualized solution. By thinking in this manner, you will reach beyond speculation to a point where insight becomes a realistic tool in all of your decisions.

To visualize, begin by simply bringing to mind the first hole of your favorite course. Concentrate on filling in the details of the hole in total. Make sure that the trees, sand traps and pin are all in place. Smell the grass and feel the breeze. You are training your powers of visualization to produce as clear a picture as possible. Visualize yourself making a smooth swing and hitting one of your better drives to the hole. Feel the impact of the ball and watch it climb, rise up, then fall to the fairway, bounce, then roll. Try to visualize various iron shots, chips and putts based on your true capability.

In practice, I try to visualize every swing and every shot before I hit the ball. Doing this builds a stronger link between my mind and body and develops my visualization skills for actual play. While looking over a practice putt, I visualize the length of my stroke and watch the ball roll over the green, take the break and drop into the cup. With visualization, you will often be able to read greens better. Sometimes, as I imagine a ball rolling over my target line, it will become apparent that it just does not look right. I have either projected too much or too little break. By running it through a visualization, I am actually running it through a test of feasibility.

Mental Framework

You have it within your power to program your mental framework for successful golf. I used to approach a round of golf with grim determination, tension and fear of failure. I usually ended up with frustration and anger. I made a conscious decision to make golf enjoyable. This decision led me to the conclusion that I had to play better and I had to change my psychological approach to the game. While I worked on the physical aspects of the game, I also developed strategies to reduce tension, think positively and, in general, program myself for success. I bring to the course a feeling of calm confidence and self-esteem. I trust my swing and let feel dictate my movements; I will play at my highest level of ability.

Pre-round. Before I play or practice, I go through a set routine to prepare myself to play well that day. I start by doing a series of stretching exercises, much as a long-distance runner does before a race. I stretch my legs, hands, arms and back muscles to feel flexible and supple. The stretching exercises also give me the feeling of being tension-free. I am relaxed, but in control of my muscles. I then watch a slow-motion video of the golf swings of a great golfer such as Jack Nicklaus or Al Gieberger. I do not put on any sound; I simply watch the swings and let them sink into my psyche. The videos not only help me to visualize the swing I want to make, they also give me a sense of rhythm and tempo that I can take to the course with me. It is the tempo and rhythm that our minds capture best and emulate. In the same light, I purposely avoid watching someone who has a fast, jerky swing so as not to absorb negative mental pictures.

During my pre-round practice, I am careful to go through my pre-shot routine of getting my target line, finding a spot to mark it, check my alignment and swing as smoothly as possible. I always start with short pitches until I have a sense of rhythm and tempo in my swing. I gradually move up through the clubs, only hitting enough shots to get a feel of each club and loosen my muscles. On the first tee, I remain relaxed and confident and concentrate on my plan for scoring well on the first hole.

During the Round. One of the major problems facing the high handicapper during a round of golf is overstimulation. He frets over his bad shots on previous holes and worries about the challenges that lie ahead of him. Alcoholics Anonymous, one of the most successful therapy organizations in the history of man, has as one of its basic tenets the saying, "One day at a time." It reminds its members to manage one day without drinking. The past is history and has no bearing on the present, and the future will take of itself in one-day intervals. This philosophy can be adapted for the golfer: "One hole at a time." The holes and bad shots that preceded are history, and the holes ahead will take care of themselves—one at a time. The only thing that matters is the hole in front of you. All your energies and thoughts should be geared to scoring well on the hole that you are playing.

I learned this lesson the hard way and vowed that I would never overload my thinking by getting ahead or looking back again. I was playing in an important tournament and playing well on a very difficult course. I was two over par as I hit a shot ten feet from the cup on the sixteenth hole. There were people standing all around the green in a gallery as I came up to the green. One fellow came up to me and said, "If you make this and par in, you will lead the tournament." You guessed it. I missed the putt, three-putted the seventeenth and bogeyed the eighteenth to finish third with a 76. I lost control of my thinking. I remember looking over at seventeen to see the pin placement and thinking about how the wind would be on eighteen—all before I had putted on sixteen. As I said before, every time out is a learning experience—some are just a little more painful than others.

The biggest change I have made is how I carry myself during the round. The change involves a 180-degree move from being negative, expecting the worst and constantly seeing myself as a failure on the course, to one of being positive, confident and filled with a realistic expectation of playing well. Actually, playing well because of practice and learning certainly helped, but setting my mind on the positive has served equally well to create a good golf game. I am careful to dress like a pro, to create a subtle reminder to hold myself in a good sense of esteem and worth. Studies of schoolchildren and workers show a definite correlation between dress and performance. I feel that looking good helps me to create a positive self-image in my overall approach to the game. While walking to my ball, I try to walk in the rhythm of my swing to get an overall sense of tempo. In *Snow White and the Seven Dwarfs*, the dwarfs tell us to whistle while we work. I will sing or hum a song to myself to release tension and further my sense of rhythm and tempo. I will take in the sky, grass, trees and fresh air and enjoy being out in the sun with friends. I have discovered that golf can be fun if you let it be fun. I smile a lot and enjoy every minute while I am on the course. A bad shot is but part of the game that I will work on to correct. The bad shot is not part of me, nor is it an indictment against me as a golfer. I have made the effort to become a good golfer, and while I'm still seeking improvement, I no longer allow negativity to spoil the enjoyment of my game.

When Bad Shots Happen to Good People. Walter Hagen once said that he expected six bad shots per round. Everything is relative, of course; I know guys who go out and expect six good shots per round. Nevertheless, the bad shot, whether it be a pull-hook out of bounds or a pushed two-foot putt, is very much a part of the game we all know and love. From touring pro to hacker, we have all experienced that feeling of despair and embarrassment at cranking off a particularly awful shot at the most inopportune time.

One of the most peculiar aspects of the bad shot is that it seems to come when you least need or expect it. Oh sure, no one gets over the ball and says, "I think I'll hit a real stinker here." But if you analyze your last few rounds, you will probably see a direct correlation between "must make" situations and bad shots. This correlation is by no means incidental to the game; its frequency deserves a careful look.

A Hacker No More

Having clinically studied all aspects of golf in my program of self-improvement, I have realized that the one great killer of the good golf swing is tension. Tension indicators are not hard to spot. I noticed that as I set up for an important shot I gripped the club tightly. Additionally, I realized that my shoulder-turn was greatly restricted as a subconscious result of tension. In effect we are subconsciously telling ourselves that this is a very important shot and is a job better left to our hands. In our daily lives we trust our hands to do many things for us—write, type, steer the car, button our shirts. In the golf swing, hand action is the end result of a sequence of other bodily movements that get the clubface to the ball in proper position and with adequate velocity. The hand- and arm-swing brought on by tension robs us of proper swing mechanics and sets up for the bad shot.

You have taken a giant step toward better golf by simply becoming aware of the presence of tension in your golf swing. Once I am aware of tension, I take preventive action. As I set up to the ball, I have only one swing thought: Stay smooth. I purposely grip the club with a pressure that will not cause the muscles in my forearms to tighten. I take a deep breath, let it out and start my takeaway low and slow. The only conscious thought I have is to get my left shoulder under my chin at the top of my backswing and my right shoulder under as I hit through the ball. I simply trust my swing and trust the club in my hands to do the job. The less input that you receive from your subconscious to produce a good shot, the better your chances of success.

Bad shot prevention is important. Not only does a bad shot have an immediate effect on our score, it also affects our mental framework for the rest of the round. Reaction to a bad shot can manifest itself in many ways. I have seen a pro throw his putter into a pine tree and have to finish the round putting with his 2-iron. 1 have seen men cry, throw clubs, kick their bags and link obscenities in never-heard-before combinations. Beyond the immediate reaction, however, lie the real problems that a bad shot can cause.

As a hacker, I would not throw a club or curse. Rather, I would do a slow burn, raising my blood pressure and building tension over the next few holes. After a particularly bad shot, my next backswing would usually look like something out of a Charlie Chaplin movie. I soon realized that a bad shot brought more bad shots, while good shots had the opposite effect. This phenomenon is often called a streak. TV analysts will tell us that this particular pro is a "streak putter." We hear about hot streaks and cold streaks in football and basketball. I am convinced that streaks, hot or cold, are not the result of good or bad luck or being sprinkled with pixie dust. The pro who rolls in three consecutive birdies has the same swing, ability, height, weight and build as always. The change that caused him or her to suddenly play exceptionally well (or poorly) is one that involves the psyche.

Analysts often say confidence explains streaks or momentum. Confidence is not a conscious effort in which we become little engines that puff, "Yes, I can!" True confidence is a subconscious faith in our ability to rise up to meet the challenges facing us. All of us have an awareness of our ability to play well. Good shots and bad shots affirm or question our level of confidence. Years of practice give top professionals a strong subconscious level of confidence in their abilities. Their confidence is not shaken by one bad shot. While living in California, I watched the San Diego Open at Torrey Pines. I remember Jack Nicklaus four-putting a green at a critical time. On the very next hole, he made a birdie and then went on to win the tournament. I know in my heart that if I had four-putted in that situation, I would have just mailed in the rest of that round—my confidence level would have been destroyed. It is just as important to know how to react to a bad shot as it is to hit a sand shot. To learn about this situation, I read, studied and talked to golfers of all levels of ability. One of the finest amateur players that I have had the opportunity to play with would use humor in his reaction to a bad shot. Following a poor hit, he would usually say, "tasty," or "I'll take it!" He was actually saying to himself, "That's not me. I'm a lot better than that." On the other hand, the poor player sees the bad shot as a testimony to his ability and an omen of things to come.

The good player simply erases the shot. He immediately begins thinking of the next shot, removing the bad shot from his golfing mind. Too often, I feel, the high handicapper sets up a trial-by-judge after hitting a bad shot, convicts himself of some fault and sentences himself to several holes of low self-esteem. One technique that I learned and adapted to my game is to follow a set routine following a bad shot. I step back and make a smooth practice swing, emphasizing a full turn and an even tempo. This practice swing wipes out any flaw that appeared in my prior swing and psychologically removes the anger and tension that may have been created. I know that I have the ability to play well and that the bad shot was more of a mishap than a reflection of my ability level. After the round, I debrief myself and make notes on areas of weakness that I need to work on in practice.

Bouncing back from a bad shot is really a matter of maturity. When you stop to think about it, you are faced with two options in this situation. Do you fill yourself with anger and frustration, setting up to your next shot with tension and the expectation of more bad shots? Or do you erase the bad shot by telling yourself that you are better than that, moving on to the next shot with the expectation of returning to playing well? When great players talk about competing against themselves rather than their opponents, they are referring to situations such as recovering confidence following a bad shot. The good golfer is not a robot who repeats perfect swings time after time. He is a competitor who realizes that playing well is the result of managing both the physical and psychological aspects of golf. Think about how you react to a bad shot and design positive steps to minimize its effects on your score and maximize your enjoyment of the game.

Self-awareness. During the round, I am constantly aware of my mental attitude. I check to see if tension is creeping into my swing. If I start to grip the club too tightly, I know that I am becoming tense. As a graduate student I learned how to let tension drain out. I was able to lower my blood pressure and pulse rate through relaxation therapy. On the golf course, I use these techniques by standing still for a moment and imagining that the tension is draining out of the bottom of my feet and hands. I let all of my muscles relax until the tension has drained from me. You will experience a renewed energy and a greater sense of flexibility following this pause of just a few moments. Use it as a means of turning bad shots and bad days into a positive experience by having turned yourself around.

Another form of self-awareness I use is to keep my ego in check. When I am faced with a shot, I try to make sure that it is within my capabilities and the best choice for scoring well. In the past, my main concern was hitting the big drive no matter what the situation. I would often end up in big trouble with a subsequent high score. My practice never included putting and chipping as it was not as exciting nor as much fun as hitting the big stick.

The name of the game, however, is making a low score. Now I find myself hitting long irons from tees where I had smashed drivers well into the woods. I now place shots in the fairway of doglegs, instead of recklessly trying to cut the corner. On par five holes I lay up short of tight greens in order to score well, instead of forcing an impossible shot at the pin. Now, when I am faced with a decision approaching a hole, I am guided by the principle of producing the lowest score in the safest manner. No longer will I blast away for the sake of ego. This is a matter of maturity on the course, an area that I know I need to watch. Try to see what causes you the most trouble on the course, and ask yourself honestly if it relates to your mental approach, rather than anything physical that you may be doing.

Post-round. After the round, I like to debrief myself by recalling particularly good and bad holes. I savor the good shots and replay them in my mind in order to gain insight for visualization. For the bad shots, I make a little mental note to work on the particular shot in practice. I do not dwell on the shot nor get down on myself. If I had a bad day, I just write it off as a learning experience with the knowledge that there will also be good days ahead and that this day was only a temporary setback.

Confidence is an attitude. It is not phony bravado, but a belief in your ability to do well. The important part of improving at golf is to attain a feeling of confidence in your game. Confidence comes from past success.

As you practice and play, remember your good shots and use your bad shots to learn and improve—then dismiss them from your mind. It is the mental picture of the good shots that produces confidence. A few years ago, I had been working very hard at my game. I had finally broken into the 70s, but instead of enjoying my success, I still felt unsatisfied. One day, my pro, Jack Sullivan, asked how my improvement was progressing. I told him that I was breaking 80 with regularity, but that I was still making a lot of mistakes. He pointed out that the game of golf is a game of mistakes. The fewer you make, the better golfer you are. He made me examine how far I had come and focused my thinking on the positive changes that had taken place and the improvement that would come with continued work. It was a good lesson to learn.

11

A
HACKER
NO
MORE

As you set out to transform yourself into a good golfer, you should make a plan. Think of the cognitive, affective and psychomotor domains as you approach each learning situation. To learn the "how-to's" of the game by themselves will leave you frustrated unless you also incorporate a feel for what you are learning and train your mind to produce the results that you want.

It is important to monitor your progress, in order to give yourself constant feedback on how well you are doing. You might try keeping a golf journal in which you record anecdotal comments on your rounds and practice routines. The journal will also motivate you to keep learning. In other words, you are always seeking improvement and always getting better. You are not settling on a comfortable plateau that most average golfers slip into during their golfing lives.

To measure progress and pinpoint areas that require work, I keep track of my individual statistics. Some of the areas that you might keep track of are:

- Number/percentage of drives in the fairway
- Percentage of one-putts following a trap shot
- Number of putts per round
- Number of
     One-putts

     Two-putts

     Three-putts
- Percentage of greens hit in regulation
     Par threes

     Par fours

     Par fives

The statistics by themselves may not mean too much, but they help stop trends and weaknesses. If I find, for example, that my percentage of fairways hit starts to go down, I know that I need to analyze my driving to find out why I am missing. I am mostly interested in trends. Are most of the missed fairways the result of pushed shots or careless alignment on certain holes? If I start making more two- and three-putts, am I missing the hole to the right or left? All of these stats serve as my agenda for practice sessions. As I said earlier, I never practice without a clear purpose in mind. The statistics help point out areas for practice.

Remember, improvement comes gradually; you do not always progress evenly. Just when you think you have mastered one area, it will leave you the next time out on the course. But if you have worked hard on a technique, it

A Hacker No More

will only leave you temporarily. Practice and sound thinking bring it back. The key is not to let these little setbacks throw you off your program. Bad shots and bad days are part of the game no matter what level of expertise you reach.

Make up your mind to be an active, continuous learner. Watch and talk to good players. Approach every situation on the course or practice tee as an opportunity to learn and improve. You will know when you have become an active learner when you hit a bad shot. If you realize why you missed the shot and why it felt wrong to you during the swing, you are well on your way to real improvement. The poor golfer shrugs off a bad shot, getting what he expected. The active learner sets the wheels in motion to correct the fault and lessens the chance of it occurring again. When you hit a good shot, take time to remember how the swing felt and embed it in your mind so that you can repeat it. Let the good shot mark your progress to reinforce you in your attempts to become a good golfer.

Our leisure time is quality time. The time that we spend with our families, on hobbies or on the golf course helps us to renew ourselves in our daily lives. It does not make sense to spend this time in an activity that produces anger and frustration. This point should motivate you to practice and learn the game of golf so that it becomes a rewarding and fun part of your life. Practice should be fun in itself, not work. If you find yourself becoming tired or bored in practice, then put the sticks away for that day; no real learning comes from struggling. The amount of quality practice correlates directly to the amount of improvement that you realize. I now practice more than I play, but I find this is necessary in order to reach the level of play that I want to achieve. If you are going to play the game at all, why not play it at the highest level that you are capable of achieving?

The game of golf is addicting, but it is a positive addiction. Fresh air, exercise, good friends and enjoyment are part of the reason why the game has such wide appeal. The inherent difficulty of the game offers a challenge that is rarely matched in any other game. This difficulty is indeed part of the lure of this game. The challenge to improve is an individual and personal one. There is no team play, no strategies to devise to defeat others. It is the golfer against himself. The good golfer combines mental acuity and physical prowess in a game that rewards both power and finesse. Golf is a life-sport that enhances the quality of life for many of us.

I wrote this book with the intention of sharing my experiences with my fellow golfers. I hope that the insights that I shared in regard to how I learned the game, how the swing feels, how good players think and other concepts, all come together for you in your improvement program. I now enjoy the game of golf much more than at any other time in my life. I sincerely hope that *A Hacker No More* becomes your personal motto.